I0815434

NATIVE AMERICAN WOMEN AND THE BURDENS OF SOUTHERN HISTORY

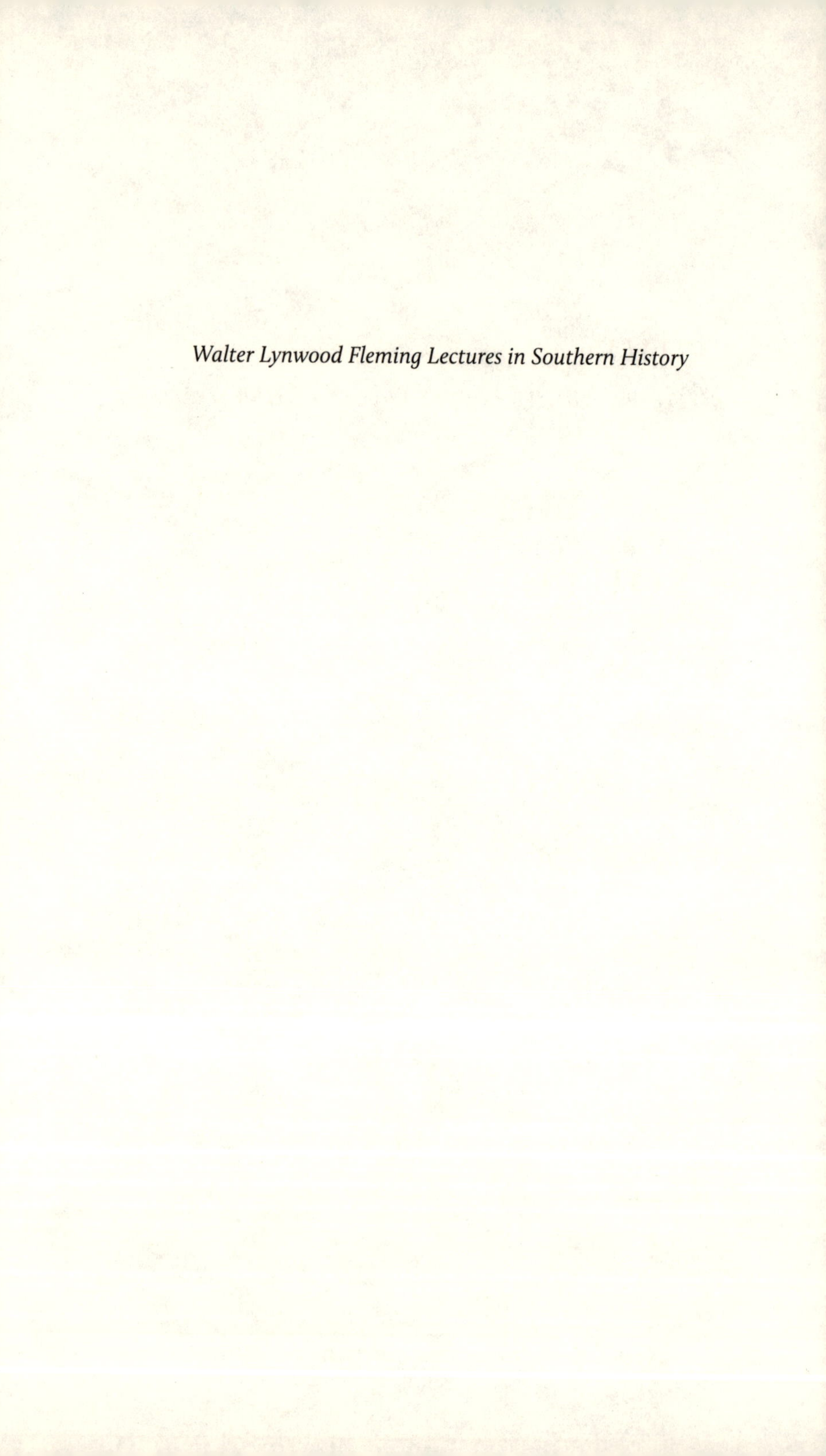

Walter Lynwood Fleming Lectures in Southern History

NATIVE AMERICAN WOMEN AND THE BURDENS OF SOUTHERN HISTORY

DANIEL H. USNER

Louisiana State University Press
Baton Rouge

Published with the assistance of the V. Ray Cardozier Fund and a grant from Vanderbilt University's Holland N. McTyeire Endowment

Published by Louisiana State University Press
lsupress.org

Manufactured in the United States of America
First printing

DESIGNER: Barbara Neely Bourgoyne
TYPEFACE: Calluna
PRINTER AND BINDER: Sheridan Books

Front jacket illustration: Choctaw Village near the Chefuncte, late 1850s, by François Bernard. Gift of the Estate of Belle J. Bushnell, 1941. Courtesy of the Peabody Museum of Archaeology and Ethnology, Harvard University, 41-72-10/27.

Back jacket illustration: Cherokee Burden Basket: A Song for Balance, 2012, by Shan Goshorn (Eastern Band of Cherokee). Watercolor paper, archival inks, and acrylic paint. Mary and Leigh Block Museum of Art, Northwestern University, purchased with a gift from Sandra Lynn Riggs and members of the Block Leadership Circle, 2017.3.

Library of Congress Cataloging-in-Publication Data
Names: Usner, Daniel H., author.
Title: Native American women and the burdens of southern history / Daniel H. Usner.
Other titles: Walter Lynwood Fleming lectures in southern history.
Description: Baton Rouge : Louisiana State University Press, [2023] | Series: Walter Lynwood Fleming lectures in southern history | Includes bibliographic references and index.
Identifiers: LCCN 2023004089 (print) | LCCN 2023004090 (ebook) | ISBN 978-0-8071-7991-8 (cloth) | ISBN 978-0-8071-8068-6 (pdf) | ISBN 978-0-8071-8067-9 (epub)
Subjects: LCSH: Indian women—North America—History. | Indian women—North America—Social life and customs. | Indian women—North America—Social conditions. | Indian women—Material culture—North America. | Sovereignty. | Indian baskets—Southern States. | Southern States—History.
Classification: LCC E98.W8 U86 2023 (print) | LCC E98.W8 (ebook) | DDC 975.004/97—dc23/eng/20230223
LC record available at https://lccn.loc.gov/2023004089
LC ebook record available at https://lccn.loc.gov/2023004090

For Peter H. Wood and Theda Perdue,
two friends who have done more than anyone else I know to redirect historical study of the American South in important ways while showing through their own words and actions why that matters today.

CONTENTS

ILLUSTRATIONS

NATIVE AMERICAN WOMEN AND THE BURDENS OF SOUTHERN HISTORY

INTRODUCTION

In June 1899 the *New Orleans Daily Picayune* ran a story about a case being heard at the U.S. Fifth Circuit Court. Chitimacha Indians were charging a group of Bayou Teche sugar planters with unlawful possession of tribal lands. The defendants counterclaimed that "there is not and never has been any nation known to and recognized by the United States as the Tchetimacha Indians with right to sue . . . in the courts of the United States." Trial proceedings had dragged on for more than a year, but over that stretch of time some baskets made by Chitimacha women appeared in the courtroom and perhaps received wider attention than the case itself. And indeed, that *Picayune* article not only summarized issues contested in the case, but—along with sketches of four tribal members—also acclaimed that "baskets made by the Chetimaches are very pretty, ranging in size from large baskets for ordinary domestic use, to small fancy ones, to be used in the sewing-room, or to ornament the bric a brac table."[1] Although the Indians lost the land claim in question, a question to raise here is why Indian baskets—of all things—seemed to matter in a battle over rights deep in the Jim Crow South. Applying close scrutiny to ways that Native American women had for generations deployed that particular feature of material culture on behalf of their communities' needs and pursuits just might at least suggest some answers.

Hopefully by now, one no longer needs to convince other historians that Native American and Indigenous Studies is an integral, albeit complicating, part of what we call "southern history." As Theda Perdue announced in her Southern Historical Association presidential address in 2011, "Indians provide us with an opportunity to examine different experiences and perspectives in the history of the South, ones that do not follow the standard narrative but instead promise both to challenge and to enrich it." But even as author of the landmark *Cherokee Women: Gender and Culture Change* who has, since that book's publication, contributed more than any other scholar to the history of Native American women in the South, Perdue does not hesitate to note currently that plenty of work remains undone.[2] Of course, our understanding of southern history has already been advanced in countless ways thanks to various studies of women and gender. Enslaved women's everyday resistance to slavery, their importance as skilled cooks from colonial times onward, the political agency of enslaved and poor white women during the Civil War, and Black women's resourceful move from domestic labor to more lucrative work by the mid-twentieth century are just a few notable examples. And in the words of Stephanie Camp, "women's history does not merely add to what we know, it changes what we know and how we know it." So what about Native American women? What might attention to their agency—political as well as social and economic—contribute to revision as well as expansion of what we know about southern history?[3]

Within the field of Native American and Indigenous Studies, of course, growing attention to female agency is also making a difference and not only because it deepens our understanding of American Indian culture and history. As Rebecca Kugel and Lucy Murphy have observed, "the field of women's history can also benefit greatly from more culturally accurate interpretations of Native women's experiences." By illuminating the lives of American Indian women, we can finally capture the complementary relations between men and women and even the complex construction of gender that existed among Indigenous peoples. Consequently, the tendency to see Native societies as simply an alternative to Euroamerican patriarchy will diminish. And as highlighted by Michelle LeMaster, studies of the Native South have already produced some of the most original work along these lines.[4] New scholarship clearly demonstrates that there is no excuse for the invisibility of women that persisted for too long in historical studies. Even when dismissed or denigrated in documentation produced by white observers and participants, their presence and influence are evident in political as well as in social and economic settings. There is nonetheless also a need to draw evidence from sources less familiar to historians. Indigenous people's own traditions as narrated and practiced are essential, but we should also not neglect visual images and material culture that reflect the complex roles that Native women have played in response to colonization and dispossession. Brooke Bauer's recently published book, *Becoming Catawba,* remarkably represents what can be accomplished when all of these lines of inquiry are woven together.[5]

My placing the phrase "burdens of southern history" in the title of this book is in part meant to be evocative, although by no means can I match the depth and breadth of what C. Vann Woodward meant by the South's burdened past. It is worth noting, however, that his list of the region's distinctive historical experiences did not include colonization of American Indian homelands—a theme that, as Angela Pulley Hudson has noted, can help us connect the South with the hemisphere as well as with the nation in accordance with Woodward's overall purpose.[6] In my centering of Indigenous experience within southern history, the particular "burdens" concerning me here will be the everyday obligations and challenges that Native American women confronted as their nations over generations were swept by waves of invasion and exploitation—like that facing those Chitimachas featured in the *New Orleans Daily Picayune.* These were burdens added to those borne more generally by most women of their times, and—as will be explained throughout this book—they must not be mistaken for what non-Native commentators too often misrepresented as female drudgery suffered under Native norms. So how did the early shocks of European colonization, the expansion of a plantation economy, and then the ascendance of Jim Crow rule affect Indigenous women directly? And of equal if not greater importance, how did Indigenous women influence the initiatives and responses taken by their people as they navigated their way through those perilous times?

To address those questions, my choice of one part of the American South—the Lower Mississippi Valley—seems simple. I grew up in Louisiana and concentrated on Gulf Coast history throughout my career. And most recently, I have found in basketry produced by the region's Native women immense material and metaphorical value. One type of basket in particular is the more substantial source for my choice of the word "burden." Throughout the Gulf Coastal South over centuries of time, Indigenous women carried large pack-baskets made of rivercane held around their foreheads or shoulders by a leather strap, also known as burden baskets (figs. 1 and 2). Therefore, the cultural object named *kish'e* in the Choctaw language visually represents knowledge and work that went into women's resourceful and consequential confrontation with seemingly endless incursions. But as you will read and see in this book, the fuller variety of Indian basketry also appears in my telling—baskets made for harvesting food and medicinal plants, for sifting and storing them, for use in ceremonial and day-to-day purposes, and, yes, for carrying goods and children. And thanks to years of careful work by anthropologists H. F. "Pete" Gregory and Dayna Bowker Lee, we have learned much about how Native Americans in the Lower Mississippi Valley have made, used, and marketed basketry.[7]

Although still underused, sometimes even abused, by historians, material culture can become a useful documentary source. In her recent book, *All That She Carried,* Tiya Miles has masterfully shown us how much there is to learn when objects are carefully put into conversation with other sources. In my own work, baskets have lately drawn me to the resilient role played by women in securing Indigenous identity, sovereignty, and territory in the American South. To quote from Cherokee scholar Rayna Green, "They tell histories."[8] And as explained in an early Americanist forum organized and edited by Alyssa Mt. Pleasant, Caroline Wigginton, and Kelly Wisecup, careful attention to material objects plays an essential part in expanding the archival space occupied by historians and other scholars.[9]

In effigy pipes made of flint clay and found at archaeological sites dating back to the twelfth century, we can see a powerful interconnectedness between women, plants, and baskets that was deeply rooted in Indigenous cosmologies and economies across the South (fig. 1). Wearing or touching baskets in proximity to certain plants, these female figures depict the spiritual and material importance held by women in the domestication, cultivation, and provision of food sources. The figure kneeling and emerging from a rivercane basket, excavated in present-day Desha County, Arkansas, and believed to represent Corn Mother, has stalks of maize growing from her hands and sunflowers resting on her back.[10]

FIG. 1. Effigy pipe of a female figure emerging from a basket with maize and sunflower plants, AD 1100–1200 (Flint clay, Desha County, Arkansas). Dr. Kent and Jonnie Westbrook Collection, Little Rock, Arkansas.

Crossing spirit and material worlds, women are mediators between the fertility of plants and the well-being of their people. It was their central and ubiquitous presence in Native American agriculture, originating centuries before and shaping cultural traditions ever since, that struck early European observers as aberrant and would become weaponized by usurpers of Indigenous land for a long time.[11]

Attention to basketry allows me to foreground the role that Indigenous women's work and knowledge has played in shaping and reshaping relations with non-Native southerners across centuries of time. The material objects themselves represent an abundance of botanical knowledge and geometrical calculation, not to mention laborious harvesting, meticulous processing, and dexterous weaving. The foods and medicines gathered, carried, stored, and peddled in those fibrous containers were essential not only for their own people's well-being, but for that of early colonial inhabitants'—an influence on the regional economy that would be erased with European lies about drudgery forced upon Indian women by their own men's indolence and about their willing subjection to white men's desire. Then as marketers and laborers later on, when the plantation economy was rapidly enveloping their tribal lands, Native women innovatively adapted to change and resisted disappearance through informal exchange relations with non-Native neighbors. And by the opening of the twentieth century, in face of lethal attacks on Indigenous territory, identity, and sovereignty in the Jim Crow South, their resilient and resourceful skill as makers of basketry became a timely instrument of political diplomacy.[12]

A fundamental question to keep in mind while reading this short book is this: What insight might be gained by turning attention away from the most familiar aspects of southern Indian history and toward the less familiar experiences and dimensions? In discussion of the colonial period, the reader encounters Indigenous groups that have received far less inquiry than that devoted to Cherokees, Creeks, Chickasaws, and Choctaws. For the Lower Mississippi Valley, the region serving as my example, they include the Houmas, Chitimachas, Tunicas, and other nations living in closer proximity to the colonial population. Then in tracing the Native

South over ensuing years, the people who remained within the region throughout the nineteenth century, rather than those who were removed, become the focus. Neither the profound loss and hardship suffered by the majority of Indigenous people who underwent deportation from their homeland nor the immeasurable influence those southern nations had on Indian territory should ever be underestimated, but it is equally important to understand the distinct efforts at persistence and survival undertaken by those remaining in the South after the period of "Removal." There is plenty we can learn about and from—as one collection of their words put it—"the people who stayed."[13] And throughout my telling of this narrative, as already emphasized, the attention devoted to women and material culture constitutes another shift toward what is less familiar in the history of the Native South. Baskets represent a gendered understanding of their weavers' environment, kinship, and community. Containers skillfully made from plants—considered relatives in southeastern Indigenous knowledge—possess a value that transcends their multiple uses and that resonates through their beauty. Showing how Native American women, across three centuries of time, created and marketed basketry in adaptive ways will hopefully enhance our understanding of Indigenous resilience, resistance, and endurance in southern history.

Burden baskets made of rivercane appear often in Choctaw writer LeAnne Howe's *Shell Shaker,* a novel that spans three centuries of time. More than any other writer, Howe has rescued the persistence of Indigenous people inside the present-day Gulf South from the invading society's dismissal of their post-Removal presence. In her creative hands, Choctaws' continuing experiences inside Mississippi and Louisiana are woven into Oklahoma Choctaws' memories of a homeland they were forced to leave. All of her stories also underscore the essential role women play in the unending struggle for cultural survival and political sovereignty. At the end of *Shell Shakers,* in the aftermath of a fictional crisis endured by Oklahoma Choctaws, Susan Billy gives her daughters Tema and Adair each a burden basket that once belonged to ancestors named Haya and Anoleta. Telling her daughters, "You've probably heard me tell the stories about them," Susan recalls how Haya and Anoleta, who were also sisters, had carried supplies in those baskets during a mid-eighteenth-century war that severely tested, but did not destroy, Choctaw unity and self-determination. "The baskets were their legacy," Susan Billy says, and "I know you will cherish them as I have." This is a mother-to-daughter message that, across many generations, has carried plenty of weight in the Native American South.[14]

I

ENSLAVEMENT *AND* EXCHANGE *IN THE* COLONIAL SOUTH

Antoine Simon Le Page du Pratz, the chronicler of early Louisiana history, became an overseer and owner of plantations. In 1718, he purchased a young Chitimacha woman from another colonist in order, as he put it, "to be certain of a person to cook for us." The mother of this woman had already died, perhaps killed in the French war being waged against her people, and the father was a man in motion. He was known to have aided Louisiana's governor Jean-Baptiste Le Moyne de Bienville in the execution of a fellow tribesman responsible for killing a missionary. And to escape likely revenge by that person's family, he intended to seek sanctuary upriver among the Natchez, a society with ancient ties to the Chitimachas. But before heading up the Mississippi River, he visited Le Page du Pratz and attempted to retrieve his daughter. At least according to Le Page du Pratz, the young woman "declared that she did not wish to leave me," and the Indian father, conceding to her viewpoint, then "granted me his rights over his daughter by placing her between the two of us, carrying my right hand onto her head, and putting his own on top of it. He then pronounced several words that signified that he gave her to me for my daughter." What did that ceremony actually mean? Was the Chitimacha woman to be considered a slave or an adopted daughter? Some historians suspect she became Le Page du Pratz's sexual partner and perhaps bore a child or two with him. Whatever the case, this unnamed woman fast became a very capable intercultural broker—like so many other Indigenous women of her time.[1]

Learning French well enough to translate and interpret for Le Page du Pratz the ceremony in New Orleans that eventually ended the Chitimacha-French War, this unnamed woman continued to provide him with knowledge about Louisiana flora and fauna and facilitated his interaction with Natchez people during time spent among them. All of that, by the way, would influence historical and anthropological information about early Louisiana for centuries to come. Among the many tasks she likely performed for Le Page du Pratz, she assisted him with shipping to natural scientists back in France an abundance of local plant specimens packed inside rivercane baskets.[2] After 1728, though, there is no mention of Le Page du Pratz's Chitimacha slave, "erased" from the record as Patricia Galloway has put it. Following Le Page du Pratz's return to New Orleans that year, perhaps she stayed behind and married into Natchez society. Maybe she was then captured by the French during their ensuing war against that Indigenous nation and exported to Saint Domingue along with three hundred other Natchez prisoners sold into slavery.

For Native peoples throughout the Americas, captivity and enslavement by colonizers was an all too common part of the earliest encounters with European usurpers. The actual scale of deadly violence and painful dispossession suffered by Native Americans from enslavement in the South and elsewhere, however, was for far too long terribly overlooked by early American historians. Tended to by only a few scholars over the twentieth century—most notably Almon Wheeler Lauber, Verner Crane, and J. Leitch Wright—it took publication of Alan Gallay's *Indian Slave Trade* in 2002 to launch what has now become intense scrutiny of Indian slavery across the continent.[3] The distance we have come might best be captured by quoting from Louis Pelzer's century-ago review of Lauber's *Indian Slavery in Colonial Times.* Although impressed by the work's fine historical and technical execution and by the "wide and deep research" put into it, Pelzer nonetheless concluded that "the field exploited by Dr. Lauber is rather narrow and not of high importance."[4] For someone to make such an assertion today would be next to impossible. Thanks to works like Christina Snyder's *Slavery in Indian Country* and Juliana Barr's *Peace Came in the Form of a Woman,* we are reaching a fuller understanding of the particular impacts that colonial enslavement had upon Native women in the colonial South.[5]

This close study of enslavement of American Indians, from New England to the Southwest, results in large part from a more general expansion of early American historiography—both temporally and spatially—that began during the 1980s. For the early South, the start of that expansion beyond England's seaboard colonies can be dated to the publication in 1989 of *Powhatan's Mantle: Indians in the Colonial Southeast,* a collection of multidisciplinary essays edited by Gregory A. Waselkov, Peter H. Wood, and Tom Hatley. By taking all colonial and Native spaces from Florida to East Texas into fuller account, the book helped scholars to see the entire region as a kaleidoscope of interests and interactions. It made clear that interior Indian nations did not simply face eastward toward the English colonies; they encountered European empires encroaching from multiple directions. To study trade, alliance, and movement across imperial frontiers and Indigenous homelands, of course, requires archival research in multiple languages, alongside fresh insights produced by historical archaeologists. Such important ongoing work is giving us stronger evidence regarding intercultural relations and a firmer grasp on Indigenous perspectives and purposes.[6]

Through most of the eighteenth century, a large swath of what we now call "the South" remained Native homelands or became imperial borderlands—spaces where colonial administration wielded little power and where Native sovereignty remained. As James Axtell stated a quarter-century ago in his Fleming Lectures, though "native cultures changed in many remarkable ways" between 1492 and 1792, "both the natives themselves and the colonial Southeast remained unmistakably 'Indian' throughout." European domination of the region was not inevitable, Axtell went on to say, and Natives played a crucial role in "fashioning their own new South."[7] Students of the early South can take pride in helping to rescue the region's longer past from behind the mountain range of books on the Civil War, built up over generations, that has obscured our view into more distant times.

Most scholarship capturing the complexity and contingency of Indian-colonial relations in the South, however, still concentrates on somewhat predictable ground: the Chesapeake Bay region in the seventeenth century, or larger interior tribes like the Cherokees, Creeks, and Choctaws during later years.[8] But as demonstrated with remarkable success in James Merrell's landmark study of the Catawbas, plenty more can be learned by devoting additional research to other coastal areas and to smaller nations. In the "geographical turn" presently underway in early American studies, a magnified look *within* as well as *beyond* the colonial spaces most commonly explored by historians is warranted. Many different Indigenous peoples—whether they be Virginia's "settlement Indians," Carolina's "tributary communities," Florida's mission Indians, or Louisiana's "petites nations"—lived in close proximity to colonial communities and often had to rely precariously on imperial authorities.[9] All of their varied struggles for autonomy and territory certainly demand greater attention, and a focus on any one location can help us to explore broader patterns. Beginning with the initial shocks of colonial violence and epidemic disease, women in the Lower Mississippi Valley, as in other parts of the South, bore heavy burdens. With their bodies suffering abuse and their labor being exploited in multiple ways, they still proved central in holding onto community and rebuilding viable kinship networks. Native women also served as cultural mediators and diplomatic negotiators in alliances that increased the security of their own nations and of adjacent colonies as well. The consequences of that agency resonate to this very day.

Although we have few written records of powerful women leaders, there is good evidence that for hundreds of years Native women ruled, commanded authority, and made influential decisions for their people. The titles of women that do appear in colonial documents—for example, Lady of Cofitachequi, Queen Cockacoese of the Pamunkey, and the Female Sun of the Natchez—reflect at the very least the centrality and continuity of matrilineal descent among Native peoples throughout the colonial South. Far more numerous in the evidence left by colonizers, however, were women who always participated in diplomatic ceremonies and who sometimes operated as individual emissaries. Pocahontas, Mary Musgrove, and Nancy Ward are well-known examples in southern history. At the most fundamental level, women's role in diplomacy included hosting feasts, performing songs and dances, and sometimes even entering into strategic sexual partnerships. Their direct exchange of material objects with European traders also helped sustain commerce with the colonies while also enhancing female influence within their own communities.[10]

Into the production of goods for both economic exchange and political alliance, Native American women contributed plenty of environmental knowledge and specialized work, and the complexity of these roles is just coming into sharper focus. At an ancestral town of the Catawba Indian Nation on the western edge of piedmont Carolina, where Juan Pardo established the Spanish fort of San Juan de Joara in 1577, archaeologists have recently examined material evidence for the influence of female agency on the fort's creation and destruction. Changes in food sources and ceramics, for example, suggest that some of the Native women provisioning the soldiers were enslaved captives taken from elsewhere.[11] A few decades later in early Virginia, Pocahontas, still the most recognized Native woman in southern history, played a far more complicated mediating role than commonly depicted—captive prisoner, interpreter, marriage partner, agricultural educator, and also artisan. In John Smith's list of Powhatan words in his *Map of Virginia* there appears this translated sentence: "Bid Pocahontas bring hither two little Baskets, and will give her white beads to make her a chain."[12]

Early in the eighteenth century, a spiral of slaving raids and revenge killings across the Lower Mississippi Valley prompted colonial Louisiana to launch a war against the Chitimacha people. The spark came when a French missionary and three travel companions were killed not far from Baton Rouge. Bent on striking fear of French power into the hearts of Indigenous people, the colonists determined to wage all-out war. In the initial surprise attack of "vengeance" against Chitimachas suspected of the ambush, a party of Frenchmen and Indian allies killed fifteen and took forty prisoners. These men, women, and children were marched to the French fort at Mobile with hands tied behind their backs. There, Jean-Baptiste Le Moyne de Bienville's forces tortured and executed a prisoner thought responsible for killing the priest.

Defending himself against a ministerial reprimand for such harsh actions, the governor claimed he was following the "custom" of Indian nations. Reluctantly, Bienville promised not to continue the practice, but he hastened to warn that such restraint would "let the Indians know . . . we are afraid." Bienville reported that he sent women prisoners back to their people with word "that the French considered it beneath them to kill women and that we were angry only with the murderers of the French."[13] Native women across the early South—those enslaved as well as those remaining free—indeed did serve as emissaries between colonial authorities and their own people. But despite Bienville's claim, more and more Chitimachas were captured and sold into slavery in the ensuring decade. When peace was finally reached in 1718 (with both men and women performing the calumet ceremony), the colonists had gained the upper hand. Bienville refused to release Chitimachas taken as slaves, but he demanded return of any French captives held in Chitimacha towns.[14]

Native Americans had their own traditions of taking and keeping enemy captives, with women commonly deciding whether adoption or execution would be one's fate. Now, however, they faced rapidly changing circumstances. The French war against the Chitimachas was a part of a wider disruption created in the Lower Mississippi Valley "shatter zone" by the contest for wealth and territory between European empires. As allies and trade partners to the English, Chickasaw and Muskogee war parties were taking captives from tribes to their south and selling them to British traders from Carolina. Slaving violence consequently cascaded across the region and escalated conflict between Indigenous nations. While the Chitimacha War was still underway, for example, a few Englishmen were upriver at Natchez buying Chaouacha captives—including the wife of that tribe's headman—who had been taken by a combined Chickasaw, Natchez, and Yazoo war party.[15]

Chitimacha and other Indigenous captives comprised most of early Louisiana's enslaved workers, but Native numbers were declining and colonial labor demands were expanding. Following the Chitimacha War, the importation of enslaved Africans (mostly men) quickly became the colony's main source of unfree labor. For Native people (predominantly women) already taken or to be taken in future wars, however, slavery did not end. Enslaved women from multiple nations continued to confront the dangers and challenges faced by all women in bondage. Some of those captured during the Chitimacha War and sold to colonists at Biloxi and Mobile were brought by their owners to other places and maintained long-term partnerships with them. Two Chitimacha women, Jeanne and Marie Therese "de la Grande Terre," for example, married colonial men and raised children who became prominent members of colonial Natchitoches. Many more captives, however, were shipped to Caribbean colonies, where hundreds of enslaved Natchez people would also be sent during their nation's war against French colonialism.[16]

Whether a Native woman was being subjected to enslavement and sexual violence or whether she voluntarily entered into intimate relations with a colonial man, the European imperial gaze characterized her behavior usually in only one way. "In the capacity of slaves and mistresses at the same time," wrote Jean-François-Benjamin Dumont de Montigny, "the girls let themselves out willingly to the Frenchmen" a month at a time for a length of cloth. How easy it was for the likes of a colonial lieutenant to rationalize exploitation of Indigenous women in terms of their sexual availability and depravation—an image that operated as a weapon of conquest and colonization. Dumont went on to claim that "they abandon themselves to it without shame and without scruple," since among these nations "there are neither religion nor laws which forbid this libertinism." When two young Chitimacha women landed in France in 1717, their status as trans-Atlantic slaves was explained by one Paris reporter as a rescue from more terrible capture by tribal enemies and as a means of converting them to Catholicism.[17] The people so characterized, of course, already had their own spiritual and juridical guidelines for captivity as well as for sexual relations. And back home, even during the disruptions caused by colonization, those customs would continue operating in order to maintain kinship ties and also extend them to outsiders.[18]

Among the many Natchez captives taken in the French war, one Native American woman provided colonists with particularly important intelligence. She was the Natchez Indians' own female Sun, or chief, known as Tattooed Arm. Earlier in the century during time spent among the Natchez, Father Jean-François de Buisson de Saint-Cosme had relied closely on companionship with Tattooed Arm for information about her society's customs and beliefs. This was before he was killed in the attack that sparked the French-Chitimacha War. There is a hint, although disputed by historians, that Father St. Cosme also fathered with Tattooed Arm the Great Sun who would wage war against the French nearly three decades later. Whether or not that was the case, there is no doubt that Natchez, Chitimacha, and other Native women were instrumental in eighteenth-century diplomacy and exchange as well as being victimized and terrorized by colonial power in the Lower Mississippi Valley. While Tattooed Arm was held in the New Orleans prison before being tortured and executed in what is now Jackson Square, Le Page du Pratz managed to interview her as a source for his account of the Natchez War in what is considered the first published history of Louisiana.[19]

Another, but even more urgent, source of information was an unnamed Natchez woman taken by Avoyelles Indians during the French war against her people. When brought by her captors to New Orleans, this female prisoner provided Bienville with some vital military intelligence. Assuming that the Natchez had already been vanquished, the governor now learned from this female captive that a number of their warriors were still waging attacks. Consequently, he ordered a group of soldiers and Indian allies to subdue them. The Natchez woman also told Bienville the location of remote fields that had been recently planted in order to provision Natchez and Chickasaw war parties. Armed with that strategic information, the governor was able to dispatch a patrol of Ofogoulas and Tunicas to destroy those crops.[20] This and other cases of Native American women communicating diplomatic messages or military intelligence to colonial officials, although poorly understood by European observers, belonged to a wider and deeper Indigenous system that mobilized female bodies and minds on behalf of intertribal relations. Seeking permission to inhabit a Choctaw town as his nation's emissary, during the height of France's war against the Natchez, a Chickasaw headman offered his Choctaw counterpart "a present of several Chickasaw women." Fifteen years later, in an overture for peace amid embroilment in Britain and France's destructive contest for Indian allegiance, Chickasaws included within a delegation sent to restore peace with the Choctaws a woman from the

Choctaw town of Cushtusha who had apparently been captured. That diplomatic episode probably resulted in her return home.[21]

It is important to understand the situation of these Indigenous raiders, sent by a colonial governor to destroy Native crops. Ofogoulas and Tunicas, like the Houmas, Chitimachas, and Biloxis, were called "petites nations" by the French. They had already endured tragic depopulation caused by waves of virulent epidemics. (The Indigenous population across the South had plummeted from an estimated half million before European contact down to only sixty thousand by the mid-eighteenth century.)[22] Such catastrophic decline, historians now realize, was made worse by the violence of slave-taking and wartime dislocations. Severely weakened, these surviving Indian nations nearest to Louisiana settlements—like the small groups in closest proximity to expanding colonies elsewhere across the South—managed to form economic and military alliances with Europeans that were mutually beneficial. Once no longer considered a military threat to the colony, the so-called "small nations" made themselves necessary allies and profitable trade partners. Recovery from the physical and psychological impacts of foreign diseases and warfare required time and tenacity. It also demanded immeasurable effort from women who worked desperately to hold families and communities together.

During and after so much turbulence, the role assumed by Native women in securing and sustaining trade with nearby colonists was also essential. Restoration of exchange relations provided a way for Native American nations to overcome grief caused by violent conflict. As recent scholarship by Elizabeth Ellis has emphasized, it is important to view Indian-colonial commerce as an Indigenous people's project, as their own attempt to integrate new outsiders into already established relationships with human networks and with the environment. For this, knowledge possessed by Indigenous women, in particular, proved vital, since they helped early colonists secure sustenance at first and later provided them with specialized products. In their own villages, they prepared fish and meat fricasseed in bear oil to serve guests, along with combinations of cornmeal, beans, nuts, and fruits. They also filled barrels with "Indian corn" for delivery to newly arriving European settlers and enslaved Africans. Native American women invested into the regional economy plentiful farming, gathering, and cooking skills. Throughout the period of French rule, petites nations persisted as sellers of animal and plant foods desired by the Lower Mississippi Valley's colonial inhabitants. When some Apalachee Indians relocated their community toward the Red River in 1763, they were welcomed by Louisiana officials as "good people, being hunters and farmers" from whom "we could derive benefits."[23] Pascagoula Indians who moved from the Gulf Coast to Lake Maurepas at about the same time were equally appreciated. Their hunting of bears, still abundant along the Amite and Iberville Rivers, added plenty to the cuisine in nearby colonial households.[24]

By now, the great value as well as volume that deerskins contributed to southern colonies' early export economies is well understood. So is that trade's complicated impact on Indigenous societies and environments. Still easy to overlook, however, are products of hunting, gathering, and farming that Native people added to tables and diets inside those same colonies. Native women not only participated in the preparation of pelts for exportation, scraping and tanning many of them, but they played an essential role in bringing food of all kinds directly to colonial markets and households. Throughout the eighteenth century in the Lower Mississippi Valley, for example, bear oil made by Indigenous men and women was a commodity highly valued by colonists—mostly for cooking—and production of that trade good was by no means an easy or simple process. While the flesh and fat cut from the rather large animal's carcass were boiled in earthen pots or kettles, in order to bring a fine oil to the surface, the skin of a freshly killed deer was manufactured into a customarily used container called *faon* [fawn or young deer] by the French. The deer's flesh and bones were first crushed and then squeezed through an opening made by cutting off the deer's head. Then, with all legs removed, the empty skin was scraped and cleaned. To turn that deerskin into a cask for storage and transport, all orifices were sealed tightly with a mixture of fat, ashes, and bark. And once the bear oil was poured through the deer's neck, that opening was also closed.[25]

Demonstrating how much colonists appreciated *faons* of Native-made bear oil for use in their own kitchens, even late in the eighteenth century, a militia captain at Galveztown complained to Louisiana governor Esteban Miró about that post commandant's attempt to monopolize the trade. Settlers at that confluence of Bayou Manchac and the Amite River relied on exchanging some of their crops, as reported by Josef Pauli in 1790, for "the bladders or guts full of it which the Indians bring in." The commandant, however, was now seizing all of the oil along with venison and bear meat in order to resell "to our disadvantage, what we poor people could conveniently buy with our provisions." Although wanting to exchange the oil directly with Galveztown's inhabitants, Indigenous entrepreneurs were being coerced into dealing exclusively with the commandant. A decade or so later, one European traveling through the Ouachita wetlands could not help but notice the value of cooking oil made from bears hunted either inside the hollows of trees or in dense canebrakes. "The grease is so fine and delicate," observed Charles César Robin, "that it remains liquid all summer, although in the winter it congeals a little like olive oil."[26]

Whether it be the farming, gathering, or food-processing that benefited the colony so much, colonial witnesses who reported on Native women's work often belittled what they saw as drudgery imposed by their less industrious men.[27] They were unwilling or ill-prepared to observe the very particular ways that gendered roles within Indigenous societies complemented each other. "Only the women concern themselves with the details of housework," according to Robin when he saw a camp of Choctaws camping in the Ouachita basin. The women "carry all of the burdens," which for him without doubt explained "why they are short and stocky and not as well built as the men." According to Robin, the men appeared incessantly "occupied with hunting" and "cannot be burdened with anything that would inconvenience them." Brushing past the various "details of housework" performed by Choctaw women, this French observer cited only one: "They dexterously weave light baskets," he reported, "which they ornament with pretty little designs in a sort of mosaic."[28]

Baskets made by Indigenous women were indeed apparent everywhere, being used for gathering, storing, and carrying foods and medicines—and even for sale as separate objects. Depending upon local tradition and availability, a wide variety of plant sources, such as white oak, palmetto stems, and pine needles, went into Native basketry across the South. In the Lower Mississippi Valley, colonial observers were quick to notice that wild cane (*Arundinaria gigantica*), harvested from thick patches lacing the region's waterways, seemed especially instrumental as a material for Indigenous baskets. Its usefulness and durability would become emblematic for future generations' resilience and survival (fig. 2). During the colonization era, no one traveling along the Mississippi River, its tributaries, and adjacent waterways could pass without noticing large and dense patches of rivercane, named *pi'ya* in Chitimacha and *uski* in Choctaw, growing to heights above twenty feet.

For early European colonists, those canebrakes were as strangely daunting as were the region's watery forests of cypress and tupelo trees. When Iberville's first party of explorers ascended the Mississippi River in 1699, they found both banks just below present-day New Orleans "so thickly covered with canes of every size—one inch, two inches, three, four, five, and six in circumference—that one cannot walk through them." Foreshadowing the environmental destruction that this valuable indigenous plant would suffer, the French naval officer declared that the "impenetrable country" would nonetheless "be easy to clear." "Most of the canes are dry," he noted, and "when set on fire they burn readily and, when burning, make as loud a report as a pistol shot."[29]

At that time, thick patches of rivercane existed all across the American South, along rivers and streams, on the margins of swamps, and in alluvial wetlands. The stems of this indigenous bamboo-like plant, growing as tall as thirty feet in many places, sprouted from subterranean chain roots, or rhyzomes, that "make tangled knots," in the words of one European traveler, "which send out a host of suckers." The cane stalks often grew to several inches in diameter, and their silica outer surface made that part of the plant quite shiny and waterproof—ideal for sturdy but lightweight and beautiful containers created in the hands of Indigenous weavers. The density of canebrakes also made them optimal habitats for mammals, birds, and insects of many different species. And as immediately noticed by colonizers, the brakes enhanced the fertility of bottomlands and so indicated promising quality for agriculture. Traveling along one of many streams called "Cane Creek," William Byrd II recognized how they also

FIG. 2. Close-up of canebrake. Photograph by the author at Vermilionville Living History Museum and Folklife Park, Lafayette, Louisiana.

helped secure waterway banks. "They grow so thick, and their Roots lace together so firmly," the Virginia planter-surveyor wrote, "that they are the best Guard that can be of the River Bank, which wou'd otherwise be wash't away by the frequent Inundations, that happen in this part of the World."[30]

Unfortunately, newcomers to the region failed to grasp the complex relationship of canebrakes to their environment, something Native Americans had come to understand well. In planting fields for food crops, they often used ground cleared of cane; they knew from experience that such usage would not kill the subterranean chain roots. Instead, if the land was allowed to lie fallow after short durations of farming, the rotation would cause cane sprouts to grow back robustly. Canebrakes are actually invigorated by minor disturbances such as blow-downs, periodic inundations, controlled burning, and intermittent farming. Colonial occupiers of Native land, however, were quick to use canebrakes differently. Cutting and burning for plantation-scale agriculture scorched the life of the remnant rhyzomes and destroyed chances for regrowth. When colonists introduced European livestock, they left some canebrakes standing as an easy way to maintain their herds, but overgrazing also had adverse effects. Habitats for wildlife and plant life would systematically diminish along the way. That pattern of destruction without restoration exposed bottomlands to greater soil erosion and flooding, with consequences felt to this day.[31]

Recounting a moment when he saw a fellow Louisiana colonist cutting stalks of rivercane, Dumont de Montigny referred to them as "the ones used to make the pretty cane baskets we call '*badines*.'"[32] To make these baskets required a series of laborious steps and dexterous skills, all of which we can imagine being learned by that enslaved Chitimacha woman working for Le Page du Pratz from her mother, aunts, or other maternal relatives. Along the banks of a bayou or lake, as told in later times, Chitimacha women first had to cut the cane at just the right width and length, cutting only at joints that showed thumb prints of the Holy Woman who first taught them how to make baskets. After the canes were carried home and while still green and soft enough, weavers split and peeled them into very narrow splints ready for drying and dyeing. They

FIG. 3. Clara Darden (Chitimacha) preparing rivercane splints for weaving, photograph by Mary McIlhenny Bradford, ca. 1900. Courtesy of the Peabody Museum of Archaeology and Ethnology, Harvard University, 2004.24.26766B.

knew that cold, dry winter days made the cane too brittle and likely to break, while rainy weather softened the cane and made it easier to make the baskets.

Splints meant to be colored black, yellow, or red for different patterns went through additional steps of preparation (fig. 3). Among Chitimacha weavers, for example, splints boiled in water with hulls and roots of black walnut (*Juglans naira*) over several days became black. For splints of yellow and red coloring, a wild root known as swamp dock (*Rumex verticillatus*) was gathered from nearby wetlands. After leaving cane outside in the dew for eight nights, the weaver boiled some with the swamp dock for a half-hour in order to achieve the yellow color and prepared the rest for processing into red. The latter were soaked in lime for an additional eight days and then boiled with the root for about fifteen minutes to reach a distinctive red color. With cane splints at last ready, the weaver could begin plaiting them into the shapes of mats, trays, and bowls. They also fashioned boxes of various sizes—some double-woven with the interior wall separate from the exterior surface. The sides, bottoms, and lids of baskets were deftly woven into numerous patterns using dyed and undyed splints. Silica in the rivercane gave all of these baskets a remarkable durability and lustrous finish (plate 1).[33]

The archaeological record, along with colonial accounts, reveals a multitude of rivercane uses over the centuries. According to the latest research, construction of two mounds located today on Louisiana State University's campus in Baton Rouge—beginning around seven thousand years ago—utilized the plant in important ways. On a Pleistocene-age terrace overlooking what was then more of an estuary than a river, Indigenous people were building those earthen structures with loess sediment carried in baskets most likely made of cane. And as scientists recently learned, between the layers of earth formed over time they also stacked and burned cane plants. Linkage to *Arundinaria gigantean* appearing in plant-cell samples at a high concentration indicates to researchers that the cane was harvested in marshes along nearby lakes. So now we can imagine Native American women and men, thousands of years ago, carrying large quantities of rivercane cut on marshland back to what was probably a ceremonial center and then laying and burning the stalks on the surface of platform mounds. Higher layers of sediment and burnt cane would be added later on.[34]

Rivercane constituted an essential element in the construction and design of Lower Mississippi Valley temples and homes as well as in furnishing them with bedding, hunting tools, and musical instruments. Matting finely woven from split cane has been found at sites along the Red River that date as far back as the eighth century, one extant piece displaying a bird-head design. An excavation at Marksville during the 1920s uncovered "very thin strips of cane" that "were thoroughly carbonized and fell apart with the dirt." In the resulting Smithsonian report, not incidental to my overall thesis as you will see, archaeologist Gerard Fowke noted, "It is said by old residents that the Tunica Indians, living on a reservation a few miles from here, 'made baskets just like these' until a few years ago.

They sold them to farmers and to anyone else who would buy."[35] Blowguns used for hunting small game were also made from rivercane, while pieces were used to make music-making flutes and spiritual devices the Chitimachas call "hunting sticks." Granaries, burial platforms, and palisades were also built with poles of rivercane.[36] André Pénicaut and others noticed that American Indians even made "quite tasty bread and also a soup" from the grain of rivercane, which early European travelers found to be "very much like oats." As authors of the still definitive ethnology on Louisiana Indians put it, canebrakes were a veritable "supermarket that offered something for almost every purpose."[37]

Some of the ceremonial and household uses to which southern Indians put rivercane basketry centuries ago are described in colonial accounts of the Natchez. On shelves inside the main temple of that chiefdom, the Jesuit priest Mathurin Le Petit in 1730 saw oval-shaped cane baskets containing the bones of ancient chiefs next to others holding the bones of retainers who had been executed upon the deaths of those chiefs. On a separate shelf were "many flat baskets very gorgeously painted," which held what Le Petit considered "their Idols": figures of men and women made of clay or stone, heads and tails of serpents, stuffed owls, pieces of crystal, and jaw-bones of large fish. Natchez medicine men also possessed small baskets to "keep what they call their Spirits, that is to say, small roots of different kinds, heads of owls, small parcels of the hair of fallow-deer, some teeth of animals, some small stones or pebbles, and other similar trifles."[38] Dumont de Montigny witnessed additional uses of rivercane baskets. He recounted how in one harvest ceremony the Great Chief received from every person "one basket of grain, beans, potatoes, or squash," and he marveled that "these baskets are of such a size that only two of them fill up a barrel containing 120 quarts."[39]

Although they are seldom found in archaeological sites or estate inventories, there is little doubt that Native American baskets, along with foodstuffs, circulated into colonial hands and households across the early South. It was not uncommon for Indigenous diplomats to present baskets, among other cultural objects, as gifts to their colonial counterparts. Exchanging baskets for trade goods, however, was a more ordinary occurrence. For example, Indigenous basketry figures in a petition for redress

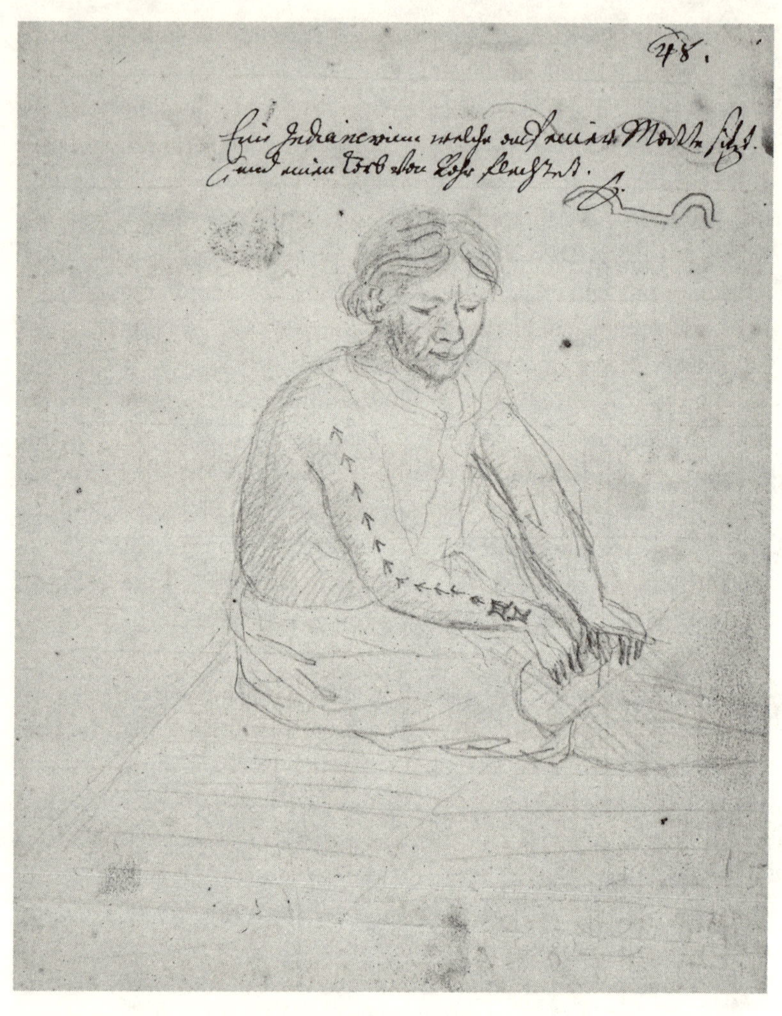

FIG. 4. *An Indian Woman Weaving a Basket of Reed,* 1736, by Philip Georg Friedrich von Reck. Courtesy of the Royal Library, Copenhagen, Denmark.

that several Cherokee men, working as packhorsemen or guides, brought before South Carolina's commission of Indian trade in 1717. Through a female interpreter speaking Yamasee, they complained that one of them had given a basket to a colonist who had promised him a shirt in return but failed to provide it. That same cheater had also asked another one of the Cherokees for three baskets, but that Native man "would not spare them."[40] Such baskets were prized by colonial elites. In 1725, when a South Carolina governor retired and returned to London, he carried a Cherokee double-weave rivercane basket with him. This exquisite example of early eighteenth-century Cherokee basketry landed in the hands of the inveterate collector, Sir Hans Sloane, and has survived in the British Museum (plate 2).[41]

Basketry woven by Native American women in and around Britain's southern colonies, indeed, received significant notice, even praise, from many European travelers and settlers, though surviving objects and images are rare. Thanks to a drawing made by Philip Georg Friedrich von Reck during his brief sojourn in Georgia, we do have at least one depiction of a Yuchi woman weaving a cane basket (fig. 4). Written observations about the utility and beauty of Indian baskets, however, are readily available—including evidence of colonists bestowing them as gifts to each other.[42] At Congaree Town and elsewhere in the Carolinas, John Lawson saw various kinds of nuts being gathered, stored, sieved, and sold by Native Americans in baskets, even confessing once to his theft of one filled with acorns from an Indian's hut. "The Baskets our Neighboring Indians make," he wrote, "are all made of a very fine sort of Bulrushes, and sometimes Silk-grass, which they work with Figures of Beasts, Birds, Fishes, etc." Looking especially artful to him, though, were baskets, mats, and boxes made "a great way up in the country" with shiny parts of split cane.[43] At the town of Nottaway, women offered William Byrd II gifts of basketry made of silk grass; however, the women's sexual appeal and vulnerability seemed of greater interest to Byrd and his surveying crew. Mark Catesby, based on time spent in Virginia and South Carolina, had plenty to say about Native baskets. Pleased with "very pretty baskets of rushes and silk-grass, dyed of various colours and figures," as made by coastal and piedmont women, he found baskets created by people living deeper in the region to be "masterpieces in mechanicks." "These are made of cane in different forms and sizes, and beautifully dyed black and red with various figures." Useful as bowls and dishes because of their very tight weaving, as Catesby reported, those formed into covered boxes appealed especially to English colonists for keeping stored items dry.[44]

Double-woven baskets made by Cherokee women were, in the opinion of James Adair, "the handsomest clothes baskets I ever saw." As he described in wonder, "they divide large swamp canes into long, thin, narrow splinters, which they dye of several colours, and manage the workmanship so well, that both the inside and outside are covered with a beautiful variety of pleasing figures, and, though for the space of two inches below the upper edge of each basket, it is worked into one, through the other parts they are worked asunder, as if they were two joined a-top by some strong cement." Noticing a decline in the volume of baskets produced—after spending some forty years in Indian country—Adair still marveled over how earlier in time, "those baskets which the Cheerake made were so highly esteemed even in South Carolina, the politest of our colonies, for domestic usefulness, beauty, and skilful variety, that a large nest of them cost upwards of a moidore [a Portuguese gold coin worth about thirty shillings]." Nested sets of eight to ten baskets, with the outside one usually measuring a foot deep, a foot and a half wide, and nearly a yard long, had apparently been a common product for exchange.[45]

In French Louisiana, Lieutenant Dumont referred to "little pieces" of basketwork sold by Indians to the French, and he described how colonial inhabitants, free and enslaved alike, made bread from rice and corn. After pounding the grain in wooden mortars, they passed the flour "through fine sieves made from slivers of cane, the work of Indian women of the country, which they have brought to the height of perfection."[46] Such precise documentation remains rare not because Native basketry purchased by colonists was the exception, but instead because its usage seemed so normal in many areas. These woven containers and implements became such commonplace items of everyday life that they were often obtained, worn out, and replaced without comment. (Similarly, Low country fanner baskets, woven by enslaved South Carolinians and used to winnow rice, were also ubiquitous in colonial times. Battered and set aside after constant use, they too were discarded and replaced on a regular basis with little notice.) The fact that baskets are biodegradable—especially in the South's humid environment—reduces the chance of their survival over centuries and explains their relative scarcity in the material record.

Despite these limitations, some testimony to the circulation of Indigenous baskets in the early exchange economy does occasionally appear. In one reported burglary of a New Orleans home in 1744, for example, there is mention of money being taken from "a small Indian basket."[47]

When William Dunbar escorted naturalist William Bartram upriver to his plantation in Baton Rouge in 1775, he made sure to stop at the nearby Alabama village and purchase "some baskets and earthen-ware, the manufactures of these people"—indicating for us that trade between Indians and colonists indeed still mattered.[48] The Lower Mississippi Valley briefly observed by William Bartram in the mid-1770s, however, was a world now entering a vortex of unprecedented changes. This perfect storm included the departure of France following the Seven Years' War and division of the region between the British and Spanish empires. Add to that the accelerating waves of immigration by new settler groups; the importation of enslaved people of African origin or descent; and the outbreak of anticolonial revolution along the Atlantic seaboard. All of those conditions combined to set in motion a series of new challenges and opportunities, both for Louisiana's resident white population and for the region's Indigenous inhabitants. After generations of decline, this is when the population of petites nations in colonial Louisiana actually grew in size and diversity. Several groups departed from what became the British colony of West Florida and moved into what became the Spanish colony of Louisiana—all in order to perpetuate an economic and political network that was important to them. Apalachees, Alabamas, Mobilians, Pascagoulas, Chactos, and Biloxis—sharing with groups already in Spanish Louisiana a background of devastating disease and violence since the arrival of Europeans—now left the Gulf Coast area between Mobile and Biloxi Bays and eventually resettled in the Rapides district of central Louisiana. The flexibility in alliance and kinship formation practiced for so long by the region's small Indigenous polities, with women obviously playing an essential role, continued to facilitate interaction with other Native and non-Native groups. And a trade jargon based mostly on the Choctaw language and known as Mobilian became more widely used than ever.[49]

Although further French enslavement of Native Americans had halted across most of the Lower Mississippi Valley by midcentury, the purchase and sale of Indigenous people nevertheless continued under lax enforcement of the ambiguous French codes that had permitted Indian bondage in the first place. Enslavement of both Africans and Native Americans had occurred throughout the southern colonies for generations, first in Virginia and Florida, then especially in South Carolina. In Louisiana, as elsewhere, the intermingling of cultures within early slave quarters created a common ground, as did the struggle for freedom waged by people of mixed descent born on plantations and in cities.[50] Now, however, Spain's prohibition of Indian slavery became law in Louisiana, and African American bondage escalated as the region's plantation agriculture expanded. As a result, remnants of the common experience shared by enslaved Indian and Black workers would dissolve sooner rather than later. Suddenly, Louisiana slaveowners faced a rash of lawsuits for Native American freedom, mostly filed by enslaved women of Indian origin or descent. These suits against owners sought to pressure Spanish authorities to enforce manumission for Indigenous slaves. In one of those cases a well-known defendant, Julien Poydras at Pointe Coupée, asserted that French colonists in Louisiana, unlike their Spanish counterparts elsewhere, "never made war against the Indians except in self defense." Facing the court in 1793, Poydras stated that, instead of reducing Indians to slavery, the French had actually "fixed all their sights on commerce" with them and "concentrated all their forces on conciliation and friendship."[51] The argument was hardly original, but it was a slippery piece of disinformation that would become a popular assumption in Southern culture, and in American history more broadly.

For Native peoples in what had been French Louisiana, the Mississippi River after 1762 became a border between Spanish and British colonies. At first, this new reality presented many with a fresh opportunity: the chance to navigate between empires in pursuit of their own interests. Their back-and-forth negotiation, always eluding one side or the other's demand for exclusive allegiance, was predictably interpreted by colonial officials on both sides not as neutrality but as "fickleness" and "weakness." From the Indigenous point of view, nevertheless, this was an innovative way to optimize their autonomy and increase their commerce. Predictably, women continued to participate in diplomatic engagements and ceremonies that were occurring at a faster pace. Likewise, they provided essential knowledge and labor in the effort to maintain an exchange network that seemed more promising than ever. With the outbreak of the American Revolution and Spain's war against Britain, however, colonial reliance on Indian men as vital allies suddenly intensified. In his military campaigns against British towns and forts, Louisiana governor Bernardo de Gálvez deployed fighters from the Houma, Alabama, and other local tribes. And when British loyalists waged a revolt after the Spanish seized the fort at Natchez—a half century after the Natchez Indians had waged their war against the French—Apalachee, Pascagoula, and Alabama warriors assisted in retaking it for Spain.[52]

No doubt Gálvez was also seeking Indigenous support, or at the least neutrality, in an order he issued in 1777. His decree commanded "all settlers to bother in no way the Chitimacha of Grande Terre in the establishment they occupy," and it directed local officials "to set to it and to preserve them full ownership of their land." Although vague, this statement came closer than anything received by the region's other petites nations in granting written protection for a portion of their homeland. For the Tunicas, Houmas, and other tribes, guarantees offered by Spanish governors would prove to be even more nebulous and unreliable. Although Spain's imperial law contained uniform rules for the protection of Native towns and a league of land around each—against disturbance or dispossession by colonists—implementation and enforcement by local officials were especially uneven in Louisiana.[53]

Despite the political leverage still possessed by the Lower Mississippi Valley's Indigenous nations at that time, the pressures of an expanding plantation economy continued to intensify. Encroachment on Native land accelerated, and commerce in peltry collected and processed by Native people fell into decline. Consequently, drawing new colonists into the familiar and traditional networks of trade became less and less likely.

Instead of things like foodstuffs and deerskins previously wanted from Native producers, a growing and sprawling colonial population now demanded the very fields, forests, and waters from which those things were harvested. And after 1783, whatever diplomatic advantage had been gained over the preceding two decades dropped precipitously with political envelopment first by Spain and then by the United States. For larger interior tribes like the Choctaws and Chickasaws, treaties would at least constitute some recognized title to diminishing homelands. In sharp contrast, however, the new U.S. federal government overlooked the petites nations entirely and left them without treaties of any kind.

As commerce with Native Americans declined in value, and as shifting geopolitics rapidly left Indigenous people behind, their recent history became increasingly obscure. Successive generations of historians overlooked two vital earlier developments: Indigenous enslavement during Louisiana's earliest years and then the beneficial exchange relationship between Indians and colonists that ensued. Hopefully, with its focus on Native women, this chapter has uncovered—borrowing words from Ralph Ellison—some light "hidden under a basket of myths."[54] Indigenous people of the Lower Mississippi Valley who had been called "petites nations" through most of the eighteenth century and were expected to vanish sometime soon actually survived as autonomous communities still holding onto scattered pieces of Native land. Now heading into the nineteenth century, what mattered most for them and for Indigenous people in other parts of the American South was the pressing challenge of how to survive after the decline of a centuries-old network of political and material exchange. Could they pursue alternative forms of trade and diplomacy that might maintain a presence in their homeland? And in such an undertaking, what role in particular would women play?

2

DISPOSSESSION *AND* SURVIVAL *IN THE* PLANTATION SOUTH

In October of 1808, William Claiborne reported to President Thomas Jefferson that the Territory of Orleans was inhabited by "many little tribes to whose happiness and prosperity" he would like to contribute. Though the federal government saw no need to make treaties with any of them, which would have severe consequences for their future, the territorial governor did express interest in how Lower Mississippi Valley Indians still made a living. "With these Tribes," as Claiborne wrote, "hunting continues a favorite pursuit; Agriculture and the raising of stock are but partially attended to; But the men are often useful, in assisting Boats in navigating the Mississippi and its waters." The women, he notably added, "have of late turned their attention to manufactures. They make a variety of Baskets and mats which are exchanged with the white Citizens for provisions and clothing. I have obtained a Basket and a mat manufactured by the Attakapas Indians, which are transmitted."[1]

That sample of Louisiana Indian basketry sent by Claiborne to Jefferson joined innumerable Native cultural objects then being assembled by the president. How the governor actually "obtained" the basket and mat and what happened to them once in the president's hands are both unknown. However, what we do know now—and as perhaps sensed by Claiborne then—is that they marked a pattern of livelihood becoming important to many southern Indian communities as pressures on their land intensified. Throughout the eighteenth century, as emphasized in the previous chapter, Indigenous people had contributed significantly to the colonial economy of the Lower Mississippi Valley, providing foodstuffs and housewares for local consumption as well as deerskins and other furs for exportation—with women contributing in immeasurable ways.

But now, amid perils to Indigenous territory wrought by the invasive plantation economy at the end of the eighteenth century, acquisition of Louisiana by the government represented by Claiborne would prove equally threatening to Native political sovereignty. Because American Indian nations in what became Orleans Territory and eventually the state of Louisiana were so small in population and scattered in location, they now faced a regime no longer needing their alliance or commerce but wanting possession of their land and its resources instead. Article Six in the purchase treaty with France recognized some Native rights, promising "to execute Such treaties and articles as may have been agreed between Spain and the tribes and nations of Indians." And when Congress organized the purchase into territories, it extended to all tribes residing in Louisiana a law that guaranteed regulation of trade and commerce for all Indian nations and that assumed the federal government's exclusive right to purchase whatever remained of their land.[2] But though the United States utilized treaties to demarcate and purchase lands belonging to more populous Indian nations in Mississippi and other parts of the South, it saw no need to do so with Louisiana's petites nations. Days of exchanging gifts and engaging in calumet ceremonies were over.

The absence of federal recognition and loss of geopolitical leverage made smaller Indian nations across the South extremely vulnerable to land-hungry planters. Where peaceful trade between Indians and settlers had once been the reported norm, complaints accusing Indians of thievery and livestock destruction now rose from the mouths and pens of citizens. In Louisiana, beginning during late Spanish rule and accelerating after U.S. acquisition, mounting pressure resulted in more than forty transfers of land by Atakapa, Chitimacha, Pascagoula, Tunica, and other Native communities to merchants and other private buyers using questionable means to convert trade debts into land sales.[3] Pinched between plantations along the Mississippi River, the Houmas began moving their communities toward coastal wetlands around Bayous Lafourche and Terrebonne. The Tunicas, along with Biloxi and Ofo Indians, resettled from the Pointe Coupée area into the Red River Valley, while some Choctaws who had begun migrating west of the Mississippi during the Spanish period also regrouped in central Louisiana. All faced in common a refusal by the federal government to recognize "grants" of tribal land vaguely made by Spanish officials. In a contest between white men challenging the legality of each other's purchases, the Chitimachas along Bayou Teche would eventually have their claim acknowledged by the U.S. Supreme Court, but as privately rather than tribally owned land still left unprotected against alienation.[4]

History of Native Americans in the South, as we might expect, continues to feature the policy and experience known as "Indian Removal." The U.S. government's removal of the region's most populous nations during the 1830s and 1840s was certainly the most traumatic and visible manifestation of Indigenous migration across the South, and our knowledge of that awful deportation from Native homelands—as shown lately in prize-winning books by Claudio Saunt and Samantha Seeley—continues to deepen and expand.[5] But while our grasp on how expansion of the plantation economy drove the government's removal policy becomes stronger, we still have a weak hold on how that economy continued to burden those southern Indians who for one reason or another managed to avoid that form of removal. In fixing attention exclusively on elimination of Native societies by what is now widely called settler colonialism, we might overlook resourceful forms of survival in the face of dispossession as well as recurrent forms of colonial aggression that continued to affect the lives of Indigenous people. Although most Native Americans, along with their governments, were forced to carry their struggles against colonialism outside their ancient homelands, a sizable number remained to fight for survival and sovereignty inside a post-Removal South. Ignoring or dismissing the presence of Indigenous people in a space one assumes they left behind disavows them of an agency and relevance that continued to shape their future.[6]

Reasons for post-Removal persistence of Indigenous communities inside their southern homelands ranged widely and depended on an array of circumstances. The smallest groups scattered between Maryland and Louisiana were simply ignored. Among the larger nations targeted by removal, most notably Cherokees and Seminoles, some members found sanctuary along the edges of lost territory. Many Choctaw families, deciding to remain in Mississippi rather than follow their tribal government to Indian Territory, awaited delivery on a promise made in the Treaty of Dancing Rabbit Creek that they would receive individual allotments of land—a promise that went unfulfilled. Creek people in south Alabama who had split from the main body of the Creek nation, before most of that nation's people were exiled to Indian territory, were living on parcels of land received for their allegiance to the U.S. government during the Creek War. As laborers, sharecroppers, tenant farmers, and/or trade partners, people belonging to these communities came to rely upon personal relationships formed with non-Native neighbors in order to remain in their homelands—always facing uncertainty about their citizenship and land claims as well as the possibility of being deported by government officials. Altogether they were becoming, as recently put by Jane Dinwoodie, "pockets of survivance where American policy makers fought to erase their existence."[7]

When it came to "erasing" Native Americans' existence, the federal government of the United States certainly deployed a variety of means throughout the nineteenth century, with dispossession and assimilationism exerted upon treaty nations being the most familiar. Less understood although equally important, however, was refusal to extend administrative protection to groups whose identity as Native American the Office of Indian Affairs doubted or denied. Government inaction, in other words, could be as damaging as government action. Pueblos in the Southwest and Native Alaskans, as well as many nations in southern and northeastern states, fell into this category.[8] But while the federal government pursued multiple ways to "remove" them from the South, Indigenous people were themselves attempting their own forms of improvisation in order to stay. This face-off in versatility was certainly not an equal one, with the disparity in power widening each day, but the Indigenous efforts warrant attention (plate 3).

With homelands eroding fast and essential resources threatened in the plantation South, Indigenous people across the Lower Mississippi Valley began to weave strands of an unraveling network into a new pattern of livelihood and interaction. In places densely populated by non-Native people, this is how Native American communities just might manage to stay within their ancestral homelands. By providing particular kinds of goods and services on the edges of plantation and urban society, especially on an itinerant basis, they could prolong their earlier role in the regional trade system and preserve their knowledge of the environment. But in order to maintain spiritual as well as material connection to their homeland, ways of preserving cultural tradition through work on land and water had to be more intentional than ever before. Possessing knowledge essential for those objectives, Native women's role as "culture bearers" would become more crucial than ever. Putting their hands onto rivercane and other vegetation that went into their baskets was nothing less than an enactment of sovereignty.[9]

In order to maintain vital ties to relatives as well as resources, Choctaws who were denied land claims and Chitimachas who were ignored by the government—resembling Indigenous communities across the South—harvested food sources and created cultural objects for sale while working seasonally for wages. Perhaps above all of the plants gathered for this purpose, rivercane woven into baskets for sale to neighbors and visitors had the most sustainable effect—involving all members of a family and community in complementary and overlapping steps of production.[10] Producing, marketing, and working in that seasonal pattern also involved travel through what might best be understood as a rival geography—a geography of resistance to the racial geography imposed by the United States. Instead of accepting exile to "Indian Territory," a space outside homelands now being rapidly absorbed by the plantation economy, many Native southerners developed a map of autonomous movement inside their ancestral territory. This was a strategic mobility that paralleled how enslaved Black southerners were creating their own spaces of mobile autonomy and resistance—whether they were urban marketplaces or maroon camps.

Caught between self-serving and pejorative characterizations of Indian seasonal movement as "nomadic"—on the one hand—and the actual displacements and relocations so frequently forced upon Indian people—

on the other—historians have been slow to recognize mobility itself as an Indigenous strategy of survival predating European colonization and continuing to this day. Since the beginning of European colonialism, words like "wandering," "roving," and "vagrant" dismissed Indigenous practices of seasonal and sustainable land use and of course justified invasion and dispossession. But we are hopefully now replacing that semantic legacy with more nuanced inquiry into Native forms of movement that might, at first glance, seem hardly a desirable alternative to forced migration.[11]

Across the nineteenth-century South, camps of extended families—units that had traditionally spent time away from their towns and farmlands for seasonal hunting and harvesting—moved along bayous and roads trading small quantities of goods with travelers, farmers, and slaves. Dugout canoes carrying deerskins, bear oil, and game to trade posts were commonly seen on rivers and bayous well into the century, and many a traveler stopped at scattered mobile camps to buy foodstuffs gathered, stored, and carried in sturdy, but lightweight rivercane baskets. These Indians on the move also assembled along the way for traditional as well as novel ceremonies and journeyed to their homeland's sacred sites—perhaps at or near ancient platform and burial mounds still standing.[12]

Effective adaptation to a surrounding non-Native population went hand-in-hand with maintenance of tribal identity and cohesion. Denied their right to land claims promised in the Treaty of Dancing Rabbit Creek, Choctaws remaining in central Mississippi pieced together a fluid economy of subsistence farming and hunting, sharecropping, working for wages, and selling baskets along with produce and other crafts. They clustered around their own churches and schools, using them as places to gather, speak Choctaw, and engage in ceremonies—most notably stickball. Some moved to the Gulf Coast between Mobile Bay and the north shore of Lake Pontchartrain, where men worked seasonally in logging, ranching, and whiskey making while women sold vegetables, game, firewood, and crafts at Mobile, New Orleans, and resort towns in between.[13] Over in Louisiana's sugar country, the Chitimachas likewise added seasonal wage-labor and craft sales to their harvesting of food from small fields and forested wetlands. Travelers on Bayou Teche as well as nearby residents found their rivercane baskets especially attractive. Among the

Houma communities in wetlands to the east, men worked as fishermen, hunters, and trappers while women sold palmetto and cypress baskets, moss mats, and other handicrafts.[14] Similar forms of Indigenous interaction with surrounding consumers, patrons, and employers were being pursued elsewhere in the South—by Cherokees in western North Carolina, for example, and by Lumbees, Tuscaroras, Occaneechis, and Coharies in coastal and piedmont parts of the state.[15] On a warm spring day in 1842, four years after the U.S. army concluded its deportation of the Cherokee nation, a resident of Knoxville walking along the banks of the Tennessee River met a small encampment of Cherokee Indians who were making cane baskets. And as recorded in his diary, they already "had on hand up and for sale perhaps 100 baskets."[16]

While Native American men in the Lower Mississippi Valley hunted and fished for local markets, steered boats and guided travelers along waterways, cut timber, or worked other jobs for wages, many Native women—in addition to vending food and medicinal plants, baskets, and mats—would pick cotton on plantations during harvest season. Choctaw people traveled to Jefferson County, Mississippi, during the 1810s, as recalled by one resident, "in large numbers," "the women to pick cotton" and "the men to hunt in the Louisiana swamps."[17] On John Nevitt's plantation near Natchez, according to his record for December 23, 1827, "Indians picked 240 lbs cotton." Throughout the antebellum period, Choctaws continued working seasonally for Nevitt and other cotton planters in the region.[18] Among those still hoping to receive allotments promised in the 1830 treaty, one Choctaw family returned from picking cotton around Vicksburg only to find a white man occupying their home.[19] Crossing central Mississippi in June 1854, Frederick Law Olmsted learned that Choctaws living "some miles away" helped harvest cotton for an employer who paid them about fifty cents per day. "They worked well for a few days at a time," according to the landscape architect's informant, and "were better at picking than at hoeing."[20] Susan Dabney Smedes, who grew up on her father's plantation near Hattiesburg, recalled that "the planters were always glad" when Indians "came in the cotton-picking season" because "they picked carefully and got no trash in their bags." Noting how Indians "did all work well," she listed basket weaving along with making blowguns and tanning deerskins as other examples.[21]

Reliance on nearby Indians for seasonal labor was demonstrated rather ironically in 1850, when citizens sent petitions calling for the federal government to remove Indians from Rapides Parish, Louisiana. The commissioner of Indian affairs, in response to an inquiry from the House of Representatives, explained that Choctaw and Biloxi Indians "are in the habit of roaming about, sometimes going to the gulf shore to fish, and at others to different sections of the country, and being employed by the planters in picking cotton and in other light labor. Their being so employed is one of the obstacles in the way of effecting their emigration to the country of their brethren west of the Mississippi." Asked to evaluate the legitimacy of the petitioners' complaints, Commissioner Orlando Brown (a Kentucky politician) asserted that if the Indians refused to emigrate "they are citizens of the States, and the general government has no right to interfere with them, though the agent has been instructed to effect their removal if they can be persuaded to go."[22]

In what became an improvisational form of endurance in their Lower Mississippi Valley homeland, groups of American Indians developed special ties with particular local families. Camping seasonally around towns or behind plantations, they regularly provisioned a circuit of non-Native households with game, seasonings, handicrafts, and medicines as well as with part-time labor. The gap left open by the loss of formal alliance with non-Native governments began to be filled by informal alliance with local friends and patrons, Indigenous people, in other words, channeled itinerant work and trade into a personal form of diplomacy. During his stay at one planter's home near St. Francisville, John Audubon recorded that on a July day in 1821 "an Indian of the Choctaw Nation, who habitually hunts for Mr. Perrie," brought him a female specimen of the "Chuck Will's Widow in full and handsome plumage." Victor Tixier, another passing adventurer with an eye for detail, observed a group of Choctaws camped behind the plantation of Pierre Sauvé, some twenty miles above New Orleans. They hunted in the area during the winter months, killing "every year a large number of rabbits and stags which are sold in the settlements or in New Orleans." The leader of this camp, a Choctaw named Baptiste, spoke to Tixier in a French-Creole dialect "which resembled the one spoken by the Negroes of Louisiana."[23]

One descendant of Alsacian families that had settled along the Mississippi River above New Orleans during the 1720s informed historian J. Hanno Deiler that "in the nineteenth century, the relations between the Germans and the Indians became very friendly." Groups traveling seasonally to the area encamped around farms and plantations and "spent their time in hunting and making baskets." The Indians offered game and other items as gifts to their hosts, and some of the white boys even accompanied "the Indians on their hunting trips, and learned much about hunting from them." Meloncey Soniat remembered how every winter Choctaws from Mandeville on the north shore of Lake Pontchartrain encamped under a grove of magnolias at the rear of his family's plantation at Tchoupitoulas. They explained to Soniat that "the older Indians who had once inhabited the village of the Tchoupitoulas were drawn back to the neighborhood where they, in their youth had been accustomed to hunt and fish without interference from the whites." "Many a time some of the Indian women would come to our home to sell their beautiful baskets, sassafras and gumbo file" in exchange for flour, sugar, coffee and bacon provided by Soniat's mother. The young Soniat received blowguns made of cane reed and other objects as gifts. Upon completion of these transactions, "The Indian woman would pack all given things in a large basket, which she carried on her back and held up by a strap around her forehead; if she had a small child the papoose would also be carried in the basket."[24]

Clara Compton Raymond, recalling her childhood spent at her grandmother's plantation of Evergreen, recorded how Indians came once or twice a year to sell their baskets. Walking in single file and led by a "Chief" wearing an old hat and blanket and carrying blowguns and bows and arrows for sale, "the women were loaded down with baskets piled high on their backs, and often a little papoose was strapped on behind." With their hair parted and braided with strips of red calico, they entered the yard and sat down in a circle. "Grandmuzzie could speak a few words of their language and would bargain for the beautiful baskets," each basket's price equivalent to the value of corn meal, flour, sugar, or coffee it might contain. Raymond's grandmother always "bought many and served them all something to eat, inquiring about their health in Choctaw language." Once all sales were done, the women filed out of the yard "solemnly, never smiling," while the plantation family quietly watched "as they plodded on towards the setting sun."[25]

Perhaps the best-known white family in the region to develop intimate ties with American Indians was the Rouquette family of New Orleans. Growing up along Bayou St. John, where Indigenous families traveled and camped on frequent visits to the Crescent City, Dominique Rouquette acknowledged that the Choctaws "obstinately refuse to abandon the different parishes of Louisiana, where they are grouped in small family tribes, and live in rough huts in the vicinity of plantations, and hunt for the planters, who trade for the game they kill." Around their own cabins situated near fences, as he also well knew, they planted corn, pumpkins, and potatoes and raised chickens. And the women, worthy of Rouquette's emphasis, "derived a good profit" from the cane baskets they made, also selling a long list of medicinal plants "gathered from the neighboring forests."[26]

Dominque Rouquette's more celebrated younger brother, Adrien, was born in New Orleans on February 26, 1813, six years before their wine-merchant father committed suicide. Following their father's death, the Rouquettes moved from the French Quarter to the banks of Bayou St. John—an increasingly busy entryway into the Crescent City where the family interacted regularly with visiting Choctaws. Louise Cousin Rouquette and her children also spent time at her family's estate across Lake Pontchartrain. The Cousin family was the largest landowning family in St. Tammany Parish, and the widow Rouquette's stepbrother, Terence Carrier, was already a trusted friend of neighboring Choctaws. Young Adrien received his education at several different institutions in the United States and France. After returning from Brittany in 1833—now inspired by French romantic literature, especially that of François-René de Chateaubriand—Rouquette fell in love with a young Choctaw woman named Oushola (Bird Singer), a fellow passenger aboard the schooner taking him over Lake Pontchartrain. Oushola tragically passed away, though, before Rouquette could propose to her. And, as the story goes, he decided to become a priest while mourning over her grave.

Adrien Rouquette's first time seeing the Choctaw community of Buchuwa, at the headsprings of Bayou Lacombe, came in 1837 during a horseback ride through the area's piney woods. A decade later, after being ordained as a priest in the Order of St. Dominic, he established a Catholic mission chapel at Buchuwa and devoted the rest of his life to converting as many Choctaws as possible. But sequestered at his cabin home named the Nook, beneath moss-draped oak trees, Rouquette seemed better at writing poetry and recording daily life than at preaching sermons and saving souls. Consequently, a friendship with Indigenous people that was much more constant and intimate than that of their other white acquaintances and allies produced some unusually detailed accounts (plate 4).[27]

According to a census compiled by U.S. agent Douglas H. Cooper in 1855, the population of Choctaws in St. Tammany Parish totaled 163 people (61 men, 74 women, and 28 children) living in thirty-three households.[28] During the earliest days of his work at Buchuwa, Father Rouquette relied heavily upon friendship offered by Kan-ho-he, who was an invaluable interpreter and a brother of headman Wellee. The village of Buchuwa, as described early on by the priest, was "a camp where log houses, bark lodges, and shingle-built cabins, with yellow mud chimneys, were scattered over a space of two miles, partly cultivated and well fenced." And in a letter written from there in late March of 1859, Rouquette reported that all of the Choctaws, except for a few, were in New Orleans, "it being the season in which they go *en masse* to sell their baskets, *gumbo,* sassafras root and other aromatic plants, so as to be back again in the beginning of Spring to plough and sow their fields, in which they cultivate corn, beans, potatoes, and water melons."[29] That community of Choctaw people, however, suddenly suffered devastating effects of the U.S. Civil War. Bands of jayhawkers and army deserters rampaging through the area destroyed their houses and fields, desecrated their cemeteries, and committed acts of personal violence, causing St. Tammany Choctaws to suffer hunger and to scatter. Rouquette did all he could to provide them with food, clothing, and supplies, even crossing Lake Pontchartrain with emergency relief at least once on a Federal gunboat. By war's end, he was having several small chapels built among the communities that dispersed because of Buchuwa's total destruction.[30]

Before and after the war, ceremonial life and everyday livelihood sustained Choctaw communities in the region. In Rouquette's account of the Choctaws' mourning ceremony, women appear prominently as dancers and singers as well as preparers of the late-night feast. And the sound of them stopping their steps abruptly with what the priest called "terrific whoops and yells" still echoes in today's southeastern Indian dances. For feasts held at least once a year, as reported by Rouquette, Choctaws from different villages on the north shore of Lake Pontchartrain and also from the Mississippi and Alabama Gulf Coast would gather along Bayou Lacombe, perpetuating a network of kinship from Mobile Bay to the Tchefuncte River. On occasion, Choctaws even performed dances for vacationers and local residents at the resort town of Mandeville and also for periodic parish fairs. Although St. Tammany Parish's Indigenous people were "adopting the dress of the white," for their ceremonies both men and women wore what Rouquette called "a peculiar costume made of calico of the most showy colors, such as red, blue and yellow, these being the favorite tints."[31] Among Choctaw cultural objects that Rouquette would send to the Smithsonian Institution for display at the centennial exposition in Philadelphia was a "fine" calico robe worn by women during rituals and performances.[32]

Other Choctaw things dispatched from the community by Adrien Rouquette for fairgoers to see at Philadelphia in 1876 (and now held in the National Museum of the American Indian's collection) were a large burden basket along with several smaller rivercane baskets of various shapes and designs. Not surprisingly, the priest recognized the cultural as well as economic importance of basketry made by Choctaw women. Observing how Choctaw men would interrupt their regular work as woodchoppers to accompany their families on seasonal travels to Bogue Chitto and Pearl River to gather sassafras, he noticed how they carried the leaves back home inside baskets made especially for that purpose.[33] And, of course, the pack basket or *kish'e* was constantly seen being carried by Choctaw women, whether on boats crossing the lake, on country roads and town streets, or at Crescent City markets. During the later years of Rouquette's life, Choctaw women arriving in New Orleans to sell their plants and wares would first visit him in his tiny room at the Archbishop's Palace. "Around him, squatting upon the floor," as one newspaper writer reported, would frequently be found "the women with their huge baskets." At Father Rouquette's funeral service on July 16, 1887, Choctaw women who happened to be in the city when he died were seen kneeling and weeping near his coffin inside St. Mary's church. "One among them so old that she could barely work" followed the hearse to the cemetery holding up a cross made with wild herbs—a farewell expression of her gratitude for the priest's alliance with her community.[34]

Choctaws living on the outskirts of Mobile also found much-needed allies in that Gulf Coast city. As was the case in New Orleans and other urban spaces in the nineteenth-century South, both the men and women from a community refusing to emigrate from their homeland regularly visited Mobile to sell a variety of foodstuffs and handicrafts. It was Choctaw women supplying homes and businesses with bundles of firewood, however, who became the most visible and caricatured Native presence on Mobile's streets. Called "Chumpa" girls because of the cry they used to attract buyers, these women often toted pine twigs and branches inside burden baskets attached to their foreheads or shoulders.[35]

The Choctaws around Mobile Bay, over time, made that borderland of their nation's ancient territory a new home and never stopped seeking some form of legal assistance. Although perceived by curious travelers and indifferent residents as simply another remnant group that would soon vanish, they did manage to turn their work and marketing activity into a network of local allies. In the face of federally appointed commissioners sent to pressure them into emigration, they and other Choctaws in southern Mississippi and Alabama found support from a Mobile attorney who wrote a letter on their behalf to the Office of Indian Affairs in 1849. Recounting abuses to body and property inflicted by some white intruders and wanting "better protection from the government," the Indians requested that "Mr. William Fisher, a creole of Mobile, who has been our friend, understands our language & wants," be appointed as their agent. Fisher belonged to a family with a history of trade and kinship relations with Choctaw people. Three years later, Mobile's mayor joined the ranks of sympathetic neighbors by first dispatching to the commissioner of Indian affairs a petition marked by seventy Choctaw men and forty-nine

Choctaw women and then writing directly to President Millard Fillmore on their behalf. The government still did nothing to assist Mobile Bay's Choctaws, but their resolve "to remain" would endure into present-day descendants' continuing pursuit of federal recognition.[36]

By now it should be apparent that basketry and other things made of rivercane were ever present in Indigenous interaction with, and diplomacy toward, non-Native people across the nineteenth century. Women were seen in the marketplaces weaving as well as selling their cane baskets, while men peddled blowguns and arrows made of the same material. One early nineteenth-century visitor to New Orleans observed that the women "busy themselves in making reed baskets which they sell at good prices." He also noticed the men's blowguns, commenting on how skillfully they were used to hunt rabbits.[37] At Natchez another traveler witnessed an Indian band serenading passengers aboard docked boats with an array of instruments made of cane. Farther upriver at an Indian encampment near Memphis, Fortescue Cuming saw the women weaving split cane baskets "of various shapes . . . with great neatness, and a certain degree of ingenuity."[38] As remembered by James Morris Morgan, who moved to Baton Rouge as a five-year-old in 1850, a group of Choctaws living on the Amite River, a few miles away, "used to bring into the town, for sale or barter, their bead- and basket-work and blow-guns made out of cane poles." The arrows of those blowguns were made of thinner split cane with a tuft of thistle at one end, which—as Morgan recalled—white boys found "apparently harmless" but in the skillful hands of an Indian proved "very deadly to birds and squirrels."[39] For an interview in 1931, an eighty-eight-year-old resident of St. Martinsville recalled—from childhood years at her grandmother's home several miles northwest of that Louisiana town—"when the Attacapa Indians traded sieves made of cane reeds for calico." On February 21, 1884, the city of Alexandria's *Louisiana Democrat* reported, "An old time band [of] Indians, with baskets and blowguns, paid our Town a visit yesterday."[40]

For the material needed to make baskets and blowguns for sale, Indigenous men and women also paid regular visits to the region's canebrakes, where, it is worth noting, they were likely at times to encounter other people using the same habitat. Hunters seeking game and wildfowl, drovers rounding up horses and cattle, and workers fleeing bondage were not uncommon sojourners through dense patches of rivercane. "As a plant of the margins," Mart Stewart aptly points out, "the story of cane also illuminates the history of the relationship between humans and nature in the South."[41] Rivercane is an especially important environmental setting in the story of slave resistance since countless individuals over generations of enslavement took refuge in canebrakes bordering plantations and towns—most often as individuals in flights to freedom stymied by slave catchers, but sometimes as families or larger groups managing to inhabit such spaces for extended periods of time. From his travels in Louisiana, John James Audubon—who indeed spent plenty of time in canebrakes hunting birds to paint—recounted an encounter with a camp of runaway slaves. It was an entire family who, while warmly hosting the naturalist with "large slices of venison" and "some fine sweet potatoes," explained how eighteen months earlier, when all its members were sold to scattered buyers, the father rescued them one by one from the different locations and reassembled them "deep in the canebrake." Also along his travels, of course, Audubon witnessed Indian women weaving baskets with rivercane.[42]

Although somewhat scarce in the written record, descriptions of Indians engaged in cutting and gathering rivercane can still be found in scattered sources. Writing about her family's plantation near Hattiesburg, Mississippi, Susan Smedes remembered from her midcentury childhood how "the Choctaws loved the Tallahala Creek. Its banks were clothed with thickets of cane which the men used for making their blowguns and arrows, and the women for making their baskets." The women sold baskets in a "peculiar way," she also recalled, with each priced at the value of the sugar, coffee, flour, and other food staples it "could hold." Because of the plantation economy's destructive impact on canebrakes throughout the region, also to keep in mind, Indigenous harvesting of cane for baskets and other uses began to require more distant travel. Over in Louisiana's Avoyelles Parish, for example, octogenarians in the 1930s remembered how Avoyelles and Tunica Indians regularly made "trips down to Opelousas" to gather material for their basketry and then carried the canes back home "on their backs."[43]

FIG. 5. *In the French Market,* watercolor sketch by W. A. Rogers for *Harper's Weekly,* December 30, 1899. The Historic New Orleans Collection, acc. no. 1974.25.20.58.

Choctaw and other Indian women carrying "on their backs" the ubiquitous burden basket, more so than the canes that went into their making, had fast become an emblem as well as a container commonly associated with the Indigenous presence in the nineteenth-century Gulf South (fig. 5). "One meets continually Indian women on their way to the city," wrote Fredrika Bremer about her 1851 stay in Mobile. The baskets, "supported by a broad belt which they fasten round the forehead," reminded her of Indian women seen in Minnesota. Sketches made by Bremer at the Choctaw community outside Mobile include one of a young woman carrying a burden basket.[44] From early watercolors by Karl Bodmer to later oil paintings by Alfred Boisseau and William Henry Buck to photographs taken at the century's end, images of this basket type abound. Although the presence of Choctaw women in the New Orleans French Market was "so commonplace that they attracted little attention" from city residents, according to Léon Grandjean, "they did intrigue the curiosity of visitors, especially when children small enough to be carried in a basket slung by a strap over the mother's forehead . . . accompanied their parents." Beside an illustration of that scene, Grandjean wrote that "many New Orleans homes contain examples of Choctaw basket weaving—round baskets, square ones, conical baskets and V-shaped ones," purchased either in the French Market or at summer places they owned in St. Tammany Parish.[45] "Towering over all" of the baskets seen at marketplaces and across the landscape, however—as imaginatively put by journalist Martha Field—were "the huge Ali Baba baskets, square at the bottom, round at the top," each large enough "to hold a portly member of the Forty Thieves."[46]

How non-Native observers perceived and portrayed the enduring presence of American Indians in the South was part and parcel of the dispossession confronting Indigenous people in their daily lives. And when reading the written record left by those observers, historians have unfortunately perpetuated views that minimize or marginalize what was actually a crucial form of resourceful adaptation. In order to understand fully the dimensions of Native American survival in the plantation South, therefore, we must demythologize a cringeworthy language used by non-Natives to justify invasion and dispossession. Perhaps above all other sights of Indigenous people in the plantation South, Native women weaving and selling baskets had become a picture of Indian poverty and decline in the eyes of most white observers. Seeing a "little cluster" of Choctaws "posted apart from" the New Orleans French Market's "main thoroughfare" in 1834, Englishman Charles Latrobe thought only that the scene represented "the desolate fortunes of their race—now strangers in their own land—and craving food from the hands of the alien."[47] At about that same time, author William Gilmore Simms—who had often seen Catawba women selling pottery and other goods around his Charleston home—was writing "Oakatibbe." In that short story about a group of

Choctaws at a cotton plantation during harvest time, Simms mournfully featured a noble Indian who symbolizes the inevitable disappearance of his race. The intricacy of Indigenous adaptation to the plantation South is thereby erased, and the Choctaw women actually picking cotton are relegated to the background of Simms's tale.[48]

Even in the hands of French political philosopher Alexis de Tocqueville, who was critical of how American Indians as well as African Americans were treated in the United States, Indigenous people were given no chance of a future in American society. "Oppression has been no less fatal to the Indian than to the Negro race," he wrote, "but its effects are different." Recounting a scene he witnessed in Alabama in 1832 to illustrate the point, Tocqueville saw a white girl five or six years of age being taken on a walk by an Indian woman and also accompanied by a Black woman. Both adults affectionately fawn over the child, who displays "a consciousness of superiority" over them, yet the Black woman expresses "servile fear" and the Indian woman "an air of freedom and pride." Through Tocqueville's vision, that "air of freedom and pride" would inevitably result in extinction. Whereas "the Negro would like to mingle with the European but cannot," he concluded, "the Indian might to some extent succeed in that, but he scorns to attempt it. The servility of the former delivers him over into slavery, the pride of the latter leads him to death."[49]

A wealthy St. Mary Parish planter, dabbling in verse, published a poem about Indians as he chose to imagine them. In the April 5, 1851, issue of the Franklin newspaper *Planters' Banner,* readers were treated to "The Maiden of Chitimachas," a condescending body of words as far removed from what was occurring at Charenton as one could imagine. James Tinker Smith depicts a young Chitimacha woman dying with a fever—"one of the last of the ancient band" to whom "God had first giv'n the land"—who is taken by a small group of fellow Indians to the shore of a lake "she loved so well." Among them was "one wild-eyed boy . . . with the bright forest glance of the Chitimachas" who "felt not yet in his bosom brave—That his doom was to be the white man's slave—To lead in the land where his sires were chief—A life without joy, except that 'tis brief." When the narrator travels to the lake to see how the "sick child of the wood" fared, he is told by her mother that she passed away. "Sees't thou yon mound, where the white shells rise," she says, "Beneath that my heart and I my daughter lies."[50]

Native Americans were a vanishing people in the popular imagination of whites who, for self-serving and variable reasons, insisted on seeing decline and disappearance. And to make matters worse, the legacy of that insistence has obscured, if not hidden, to this day Indigenous resistance and persistence in the South and elsewhere—explaining in large part historians' lack of attention. "A doomed and dying race is stirring poetic material," writes essayist Rebecca Solnit, but "a people with a talent for integrating change is not." And as Solnit further observes, picturing Indians "as fixed in time, possessed of fragile and static cultures which crumble under the force of colonialist contamination" purposely denies their being political "with a voice, rights, and membership." Their alleged absence makes them nothing but a curiosity.[51]

While the intimate knowledge of the environment that women wove into their baskets actually facilitated Indigenous survival and adaptation, that very perseverance was perceived and represented as declension. What was actually a way to express and maintain some degree of sovereignty has unfortunately reached us, in one distorted form or another, through a rather narrow vision of non-Native eyes. While Walt Whitman spent three months of 1848 in New Orleans, working as editor and writer for the *Daily Crescent,* his "choice amusements" included Sunday morning walks to the French Market, where "the show was a varied and curious one." And among the "hucksters with their wares" whom Whitman found so amusing, "there were always fine specimens of Indians, both men and women, young and old." Sharpening focus on the Native women seen at that same marketplace in the 1870s, Lafcadio Hearn wrote—even more harmfully than Whitman—"The sadness that seems peculiar to dying races could not be more evident than in them." The impact, if not the intent, of sentiments directed at Indian women, ranging from amusement and curiosity to pathos and loathing, was to erase them from history.[52]

Images of solitary Indian women pathetically peddling their baskets and representing their people's imminent disappearance had the twin effects of relegating American Indians to a romantic past and of denying them a viable presence in the present-day economy. Stories told about

Indian basket makers across the continent, as Laurel Ulrich so aptly put it, held a "doubleness often associated with people surviving in the shadow of oppression." Reflecting a tenuous means of livelihood in the expanding commercial and industrial economy, the visibility of basket selling made Indian peddlers vulnerable to the demeaning impact of both pity and curiosity.[53] Appearing pitiful or beggarly, however, was perhaps a way of expecting compensation and recognition. Like gift giving during earlier times, it was an expression of reciprocity and autonomy and not dependency and submission. No doubt, those beleaguered looks on the faces of Choctaw women selling wares from place to place and in town markets did reflect consequences of dispossession. Undeniably, however, they also helped sustain cordial and beneficial relations with white patrons and customers.

Also contributing to assumptions about Indian women's misery and despair was an insistence upon seeing Indian men as indolent and irresponsible that originated in the colonial era. "The men, when not hunting," Fortescue Cuming wrote in the early nineteenth century about a camp near Memphis, "lounge at full length wrapped in their blankets, or sit cross legged, while the women do the domestic drudgery." Surveying Gulf coastal timber lands for the U.S. Navy in 1819, James Cathcart described the Choctaws outside Mobile with these derisive words: "The men sometimes hunt, but most frequently are seen following their females who are loaded with fire wood, & often with a young child sitting on the top of the load with another at her breast, & leading a third, while their lazy husbands saunter unconcern'd behind them." The men, he claimed, spent their wives' "hard earn'd trifle" getting drunk on rum.[54] Perceptions of Indians have served metaphorically for countless messages circulating in American thought and rhetoric, so when John Pintard praised Christianity's elevating influence on female morality and status in an 1821 letter to his married daughter living in New Orleans, he wrote, "What you were in the days of heathenism is exemplified before your eyes whenever you see a poor Indian woman . . . doomed to perform all the drudgery of her tribes . . . while their lordly masters look down on everything but war & hunting with contempt." "Point out this remark to your daughters," he insisted, "as you walk the Levée and see the miserable Choctaws."[55]

PLATE 1. Double-weave basket, “Up Across and Down” design, made by Clara Darden (Chitimacha), ca. 1900. Museum Purchase, 1932. Courtesy of the Peabody Museum of Archaeology and Ethnology, Harvard University, 32-18-10/28.

PLATE 2. Cherokee basket (double-woven split cane), 1720s, received by Hans Sloane from Colonel Francis Nicholson, 1720s. Courtesy of the British Museum, London.

PLATE 3. *Louisiana Indians Walking along a Bayou*, 1847, by Alfred Boisseau. The New Orleans Museum of Art: Gift of William E. Groves, 56.34.

PLATE 4. *Choctaw Village near the Chefuncte,* late 1850s, by François Bernard. Gift of the Estate of Belle J. Bushnell, 1941. Courtesy of the Peabody Museum of Archaeology and Ethnology, Harvard University, 41-72-10/27.

PLATE 5. *Choctaw Belle,* Mobile, 1850, by Phillip Romer.
Courtesy of Museums at Washington and Lee University, Lexington, Virginia.

PLATE 6. *Strength,* 2017, by Sarah Sense (Chitimacha/Choctaw).
Woven archival inkjet prints on bamboo paper and rice paper, wax, tape,
acrylic paint. Courtesy of Sarah Sense.

PLATE 7. *Cherokee Burden Basket: A Song for Balance,* 2012, by Shan Goshorn (Eastern Band of Cherokee). Watercolor paper, archival inks, and acrylic paint. Mary and Leigh Block Museum of Art, Northwestern University, purchased with a gift from Sandra Lynn Riggs and members of the Block Leadership Circle, 2017.3.

PLATE 8. *Cultural Burdens,* 2015, by Carol Emarthle-Douglas (Northern Arapaho/Seminole). Courtesy of Carol Emarthle-Douglas.

In 1850 Lady Emmeline Stuart-Wortley and her daughter were riding the railway from New Orleans to the steamboat dock on Lake Pontchartrain—on their way to Mobile—when they saw a group of Indians along the way. The men, she thought, were "a magnificent-looking set," splendidly dressed in "very brilliant and picturesque" clothing and walking "upright as their own arrows . . . but not so their unlucky squaws, who followed after, bowed under the weight" of children and baggage. "Poor creatures!" exclaimed Stuart-Wortley. "How wearily they seemed plodding along after the ungallant gentlemen of the party, who had burdened themselves with nothing but their guns."[56]

From the start of European colonization, as shown remarkably well a quarter-century ago by Jennifer Morgan, distorted descriptions and depictions of the female bodies of non-European women across the Atlantic World had been a powerful ideological weapon of enslavement and conquest.[57] So it should come as no surprise that preoccupation with Native women's physical appearance during the nineteenth century continued to shape misrepresentation of their role in coping with dispossession. At a plantation twenty miles upriver from New Orleans, where some Choctaws were staying at "wood's edge," Victor Tixier in 1840 saw women and girls seated around the camp "busily weaving baskets of reed." They ran into their huts, however, as the stranger approached. Only after Tixier partook of a meal and smoked a pipe with the men did the women become "more sociable" and return to "their basket weaving." Describing them as "small" with "good figures," he considered them "perfectly ugly and untidy"—their faces broad, eyes dull and dark, hair long and greasy, and cheeks tattooed with blue lines. Tixier was nonetheless impressed, as he mentioned in passing, with their knowledge of many medicinal plants.[58] Attention to looks—always a distraction from the substance of women's work and mostly an instrument of domination—sometimes did paint a more complimentary picture. Writing about several visits with her mother to a Choctaw community on the outskirts of Mobile when she was a young teenager, Victoria Welby-Gregory recalled seeing "a certain nobleness of look" in the men and considering many of the women "very handsome." During one of those visits, Victoria even sketched someone she thought was "the loveliest woman I ever saw" with "a perfectly straight" nose, lustrous black eyes, a "rose-bud" mouth, and a "dark brownish red" complexion. This was, by the way, an all too rare occasion when an Indigenous woman's name was recorded in a travel account; hers, according to the English noblewoman, was Manolahona.[59]

But alas, readers at that time could find reference to another named Choctaw woman living around Mobile. In a romantic sketch written by Alexander B. Meek—a lawyer, editor, public official, and author of fiction and nonfiction who lived in that city for nearly two decades—they read about one of those "simple daughters of the woods," who in Meek's opinion were "quite handsome," possessing beneath their calico gowns and red blankets "considerable graces of manner and appearance." In 1846 a Choctaw "of unusual beauty and attractiveness," thought to be no older than seventeen and "called in the Indian tongue, The Wild Fawn of Pascagoula," was one of the most successful dealers in berries and pinewood because of her "personal charms." How Meek most likely visualized his Native character is echoed in *Choctaw Belle,* a portrait painted four years later by Bavarian artist Phillip Romer (plate 5). Among the city's young men eager to buy things from the "Wild Fawn of Pascagoula," there was a lawyer so smitten that he yearned to win her heart. As her visits to the young lawyer's downtown office grew more frequent and longer lasting, the Fawn "took an evident interest in his attention." But when he finally decided to demonstrate his love with an embracing kiss, she quickly retreated across the room and—for the first time he ever heard her speak English—exclaimed, "Me good friend to kind gentleman—but no love! The Fawn must marry her own people. She love young warrior up on Pascagoula! He have heart and skin the same color! Mobile man not good for Choctaw girl." In this predictable narrative about forbidden love across a cultural divide, the young lawyer laments, "Is it possible! Caught in my own trap! Jilted by an Indian!" And so the story ends with him whimsically resenting how the Fawn of Pascagoula had for months so timidly "taken all my presents and delicate attentions" and left him feeling as if he had been sacked by "any fashionable coquette in a gilded saloon, by the light of a chandelier."[60]

As if the wry sentimentalism dripping from Alexander Beaufort Meek's pen did not commit enough deceit, members of the same Choctaw community were also subjected to the gaze of two well-known scientists. Hosting Louis Agassiz in Mobile, physician and phrenologist Josiah Nott took the Harvard zoologist around the city to observe Choctaws who frequented its streets and markets. The principal purpose of Agassiz's visit was to find an African American's brain in order to demonstrate how it never matured beyond that of a Caucasian boy, but Nott took the occasion to demonstrate his theory that the American Indian crania was uniformly small in size, "averaging but seventy-nine cubic inches in internal capacity" and having other distinguishing features. As Nott gleefully reported the next year in his *Types of Mankind,* Agassiz's "critical eye detected no exception in at least 100 living Choctaws Indians whom we examined together." As we know all too well, the Mobile physician was committing his ethnological "research" to prove that "Nations and races . . . have each an especial destiny: some are born to rule, and others to be ruled" and that "no two distinctly-marked races can dwell together on equal terms." In Nott's racist order of things, "the Negro thrives under the shadow of his white master," while "contact with the white man seems fatal to the Red American, whose tribes fade away before the onward march of the frontier like the snow in spring."[61]

While elite southerners were formulating theories of racial difference to fix boundaries and establish hierarchy, people on the ground nonetheless continued socializing and exchanging goods with each other out of necessity or habit. Whether for seasonal work at timber camps and plantations, or for selling fish, game, and housewares, or for recreational gatherings, Indian communities regularly came face-to-face with neighboring Blacks and Whites as well as with each other. Their very survival as a distinct people spanning a century of population decline and land loss had, after all, depended upon such interaction. And while slavery more than race still marked the sharpest boundary, flexibility persisted when it came to personal identity. Nevertheless, fluid relations with outsiders—whether with slaves, slaveholders, or poor whites—were bound to cause ambivalence at the very least within Indigenous communities.

Outstanding scholarship on Black-Indian relations has lately made a significant mark on the advancement of southern history, as represented in landmark works by Tiya Miles, Celia Naylor, David Chang, and Barbara Krauthamer.[62] That scholarship, however, is still mostly framed within the context of slavery, during colonial times as fellow enslaved people working side-by-side or during the nineteenth century as African Americans owned by Native Americans. And when relations on the margins of slavery are examined, the focus is almost exclusively on interaction between poor whites and slaves. Yet the methodological challenges and observations undertaken by those historians are indeed applicable to both groups' interaction with Indigenous southerners. Stereotypes and elusive evidence, as Jeff Foret has explained, stood in the way of understanding the complex range of relations that endured since the colonial period. Although poor whites played a major role in controlling slaves and in supporting the slave regime as overseers, patrolers, and slave hunters, they nonetheless socialized with slaves through work as extra hands and through leisure-time activities—the latter in defiance of laws. Mostly involving enslaved men, illicit trade also provided a space of interaction. Similar interaction occurred between Indians and whites, but with Native women playing a prominent role as peddlers and thereby resembling Black women in southern towns and cities.[63]

Before the Civil War, an insistence on lumping non-whites as either slaves or free people of color and thereby forgetting Indians were here, posed challenges that remain relatively obscure in historiography but continue to have repercussions to this day. While interacting socially and economically with the non-Native population, Native Americans had to somehow set themselves apart from those categories in a world where, as put by Jack Forbes, "whites . . . are always finding blacks, and they are always losing Indians."[64] Because free Blacks in the slave South, irrespective of their economic status, confronted social isolation and legal confinement, simply not being enslaved was an insufficient choice for Indigenous people. And making matters worse, whites weaponized charges of mixture to undermine Indian communities' pursuit of legal protection. A petition from citizens in King William County, Virginia, in 1843, for example, justified their grab for the Pamunkeys' land by asserting that their claim to being Indian no longer existed because their "blood has so largely mingled with that of the Negro race as to have obliterated all striking features of

Indian extraction." Denying rights to people labeled by the U.S. census as "all other free persons"—in order to secure white supremacy, preserve slavery, and take Indian land—was, as noted by Malinda Maynor Lowery for the Lumbees in North Carolina, the "Trail of Tears" suffered by American Indians who averted the more familiar Removal experience. In his study of the Chowans in that same state, Warren Milteer reinforces the role played by racialization—hardly a reliable marker of community's identity and cohesion—in detaching Indigenous people from their land.[65] Racialized erasure, remember, was another instrument of Removal.

As white supremacy weaponized fluid relations with other marginalized inhabitants of the region, the end of slavery made it more essential than ever for American Indians to identify as free people of color not of African descent. Passing observers had often used phrases like "half breed" and "mongrel" to characterize Indians, routinely claiming that—except for a "full-blooded" family here and there—they were "dying out" or "melting away." Outsiders seldom agreed over whether individuals were "mingling" with Blacks or with whites.[66] By the end of the nineteenth century, with the ascent of Jim Crow rule, such racialized labeling became increasingly perilous. A somewhat extraordinary test of this was experienced by Choctaws in south Alabama, when the U.S. government held several hundred Chiricahua Apache men, women, and children—including Geronimo—as prisoners at Mount Vernon Barracks, a former arsenal located about twenty miles north of Mobile. Amid the trauma, sickness, and death they suffered at that internment camp from 1887 to 1894, the Apaches nonetheless were allowed some freedom to interact with the local population, including spectators who took railway excursions to Mount Vernon and were eager to see, and even buy souvenirs from, "real" western Indians. Over those years, the Mobile-area Choctaws developed their own relationship with the Apaches through regular social interaction as well as commerce that included some whiskey making. But once the southwestern Indian prisoners were relocated to Oklahoma, as Angela Pulley Hudson has recently emphasized, the Choctaws who still remained on a piece of their homeland would find themselves being sharply contrasted with the Apaches and, consequently, their Indian identity being questioned more severely than before.[67]

Coinciding with the Chiricahua Apaches' imprisonment at Mount Vernon, the U.S. Census Bureau for the first time included in its general count for 1890 newly labeled "Indians Taxed and Indians Not Taxed"—distinguishing them from "Indians on reservations, under the care of the government." Until then, Indigenous people not living on federal reservations were commonly identified in decennial censuses as white, black, or mulatto, only in rare instances as Indian. In the 1890 general census of "Indians Taxed and Indians Not Taxed" living in Alabama, the Apache prisoners at Mount Vernon were counted separately from what the bureau called "the civilized (self-supporting) Indians." The latter category, numbering 759 individuals, included mostly Choctaw and Creek people who for generations lived in south Alabama but who were imagined by non-Natives to be nothing like Apaches from the Southwest. According to the Department of Interior's narrative about them, "The mode of life of these Indians is akin to that of their neighbors of small property. Among them are the descendants of Creek, Cherokee, Chickasaw, and Mobile Indians, more or less affected by white and negro blood." This misleading racial and confusing tribal characterization of Mobile-area Choctaws and Creeks, which resembled how comparable groups throughout the South were also described, reflects the federal government's overall lack of attention and interest when it came to Indigenous people across the eastern United States. The Interior Department's summary regarding all those now being counted in general censuses as Indians said that "the separation of Indians from the general population in the conditions now prevailing in considerable portions of the country is exceedingly difficult and unsatisfactory. The number of persons east of the Mississippi who would suggest to an enumerator by their appearance that they have any Indian blood is very small." After commenting that way about physical features, the report went on to acknowledge that "Indians taxed and Indians not taxed are terms that can not be rigidly interpreted, as Indian citizens, like white citizens, frequently have nothing to tax." How officials counted people in the nation was obviously another means of erasing Native Americans from public awareness and denying the government's responsibility to them.[68]

White supremacy directed at American Indians on multiple fronts, although presenting a somewhat different face than that aimed at African Americans, now posed a mounting threat to what remained of Native territory and sovereignty in the South. Owner of a plantation on Bayou Teche midway between the Chitimacha community at Charenton and the town of New Iberia, Francis DuBose Richardson wrote in an article for *Southern Bivouac* magazine that "the Attakapas Indians" of the 1880s had hardly changed over the previous half-century. "They had then pretty much lost their identity as a tribe," he asserted, "though they still had a nominal chief and owned their little reservation at the Indian Bend, where about the same number of wigwams or huts stood then as now. No pure bloods remain, and the half-breeds show no improvement in the stock." In addition to mistaking Chitimachas for Atakapas (a common confusion of their names at that time), the sugar planter went on to make what had become a standard prediction regarding all Indigenous people: "As the world is now moving on the Teche, it will not be long before some Chicago capitalist will come down and take the female remnants of the tribe in as partners—as their entailed property can not be sold—and establish a first-class sugar plantation on the old reservation."

Richardson's statement was obviously an example of crass arrogance, but it also reveals an anxiety that many neighboring planters felt about the Chitimachas' title to their remaining property. If their Indian status were somehow acknowledged by the federal government, the Chitimachas' remaining land might not be as easy to acquire as were lands once owned by Acadian farmers in the area. In that same article, Richardson tellingly pointed out that "fifty-six years ago the Teche was much more thickly settled than now, for it took many small places to make one large sugar-plantation, and many of these small farmers moved further up the country or back into the prairies." Along with plantation pressure on Indian autonomy in Louisiana's sugar bowl, we should not forget, came dispossession of poorer whites as well as repression of Black workers.[69]

Just one year before Richardson published that magazine article, the World's Industrial and Cotton Centennial Exposition was held in New Orleans. A celebration of the South's plantation economy, the nation's postwar reunification, the promise of industrialization, and the expansion of U.S. power, that world's fair offered visitors only a modicum of information about Indigenous people in the South. One exhibit featured photographs of a Plains Indian people; another highlighted the government's Indian boarding school at Carlisle. Outside the fairgrounds, of course, one could watch Buffalo Bill Cody's Wild West performance of Indian battles and stagecoach attacks.[70] The fair guidebook did direct readers to "the fifteen or twenty Choctaw women whom one sees at the French Market," but hastened to portray them as "sitting patiently, silent and motionless, waiting (with some contempt, if the truth were known) for the pale-face purchaser" of their gumbo filé, baskets, and medicinal herbs—being "almost the sole survivors of the race which inherited the land from their fathers." The only representation of local Indians on the fairgrounds, however, came in the form of their cultural objects, with both Choctaw and Chitimacha basketry prominently displayed in Louisiana's state exhibit. The guidebook lavished special praise on rivercane baskets made by Chitimacha women, saying they "are really objects of art, and are highly prized by those who can secure them."[71] Catering to fairgoers' nostalgic desire for exotic things," a *New Orleans Times-Democrat* account of those baskets in Louisiana's exhibit attributed the persistence of Indian tribes in the state to its "great forests and swamps . . . which could be inhabited by none save Indians, acclimated by centuries of residence therein." The newspaper also emphasized that the specimens of handiwork on exhibit "were procured with infinite difficulty" because their makers' "intense aversion to the whites." "Only by the most strenuous and diplomatic efforts," it further remarked, can a white man "gain an interview with an Indian."[72]

In that sort of language written about access to American Indian basketry, one finds a mixture of irony with supposition that warrants our consideration. Notice how the resourceful and innovative agency of Indigenous people responsible for their survival is made to seem natural rather than purposeful. White consumers' "diplomacy" also seems to displace if not erase that of Native producers. And not to be overlooked—and possibly the most important factor in that account—is how exhibits of Indian cultural objects toward the close of the nineteenth century, like that in New Orleans, might have signaled the opening of a new kind of appreciation and representation. Perhaps on the horizon, thanks in part to widening attention drawn to Indian baskets at events like international expositions, a marketable interest unlike any before was emerging. And what remains to be seen, in the next chapter, is how Native American women would respond to that attention. Could work that had sustained their communities' struggle for sovereignty and territory across two centuries of colonialism continue to matter as they now confronted further perils in the Jim Crow South?

3

PERIL *AND* RECOVERY *IN THE* JIM CROW SOUTH

In the spring of 1905 a Chitimacha woman named Christine Paul wrote letters to Mary McIlhenny Bradford reporting that "we are in truble with our land I don't know what they want do with us they trying there best to put us out" (fig. 6). The Chitimachas' remaining 250 acres of land along Bayou Teche perilously faced a court-ordered auction in order to satisfy debt owed an attorney, who—to make matters even worse—was claiming that "we not Indians because we mix so much" and that "we not a nation." "I don't know what we are then if we not nation," Christine Paul bemoaned. "I am sure we not dogs." Within that same correspondence to Mrs. Mary Bradford—daughter of Tabasco Company founder Edmund McIlhenny and a resident of Avery Island—Mrs. Paul, wife of tribal headman Benjamin Paul, also reported on progress underway in meeting Bradford's latest order for Chitimacha basketry, following a bout of sickness among some of the weavers.[1] Since 1899 Christine, now thirty years old, had been regularly sending to Mary rivercane baskets made by herself and about fourteen other Chitimacha women and girls. Charenton and Avery Island were separated by fifty or so miles of mostly shell road (thirty miles to New Iberia, then twenty to Avery Island), but that distance was nothing compared to what separated Christine and Mary in social status and daily life. Those baskets made by Indian women, however, had drawn them together into a relationship that would be consequential for the survival of the Chitimacha nation in the Jim Crow South.[2]

FIG. 6. Christine Paul (Chitimacha) weaving a rivercane basket, ca. 1903, photograph by Mary McIlhenny Bradford. Courtesy of the Avery Island Archives.

In dynamic and resourceful ways, Native American women for generations had been confronting burdens of southern history—from enslavement to displacement—with basketry made by them along the way helping maintain Indigenous identity, connection to homeland, and intercultural diplomacy. Heading into the twentieth century, however, the weight of those burdens only seemed to get heavier for Indian communities across the South. Pieces of homelands remaining in Native hands became more severely imperiled, and racialization under Jim Crow jeopardized Indian identity and sovereignty. Some Indian people in this region even faced violence. Also over time, the seasonal work and trade that had facilitated adaptive interaction and helped sustain ties to homelands became less tenable. Local markets for basketry, for example, weakened in most places as more and more household uses switched to store-bought metal ware.

Amid all of this, the federal government still refused to provide protection, and southern state governments—showing Native people little or no sympathy—predictably preferred it that way. When in the spring of 1896, an Avoyelles Parish grand jury indicted Fulgence Chiqui for assaulting a fellow tribesman with a knife, he contested its jurisdiction on grounds that both he and his alleged victim were Tunica and that—as written in the note of evidence jointly presented by their own lawyer and the district attorney—"never before this, have the authorities of this parish taken cognizance of crimes or offenses committed by Indians against Indians within said reservation." Despite this shared understanding by the Tunicas and local authorities, however, the state of Louisiana disputed the assertion that Tunica land constituted "Indian country" as defined by U.S. law. In response to an inquiry sent by state justice Samuel D. McEnery, Commissioner of Indian Affairs Daniel W. Browning replied with music to the judge's ears. "This office," he declared, "does not have any knowledge of any land in Louisiana set apart for Tunica or any other Indians." Browning rather selectively cited an early nineteenth-century account of the region's Indian population that had counted only twenty-five men among the Tunicas back then. Also noting how they were "employed occasionally by the inhabitants as boatmen, etc." and lived "in amity with all other people," the author of that report, John Sibley, nonetheless assumed that the Tunicas were "gradually diminishing in numbers." So with backing from an age-old assumption about the region's Indigenous people heading to extinction, Louisiana justice and soon-to-be U.S. senator McEnery crowed, "The Federal Government does not have jurisdiction over any Indians in Louisiana."[3]

Considering such a convergence of challenges and obstacles, the need for non-Native allies became deeper than ever. And yet it seems most unlikely that basketry made by Native American women could survive as a sufficient instrument of diplomacy. Coinciding with the surge of threats to Indigenous identity and land in the Jim Crow South, however, was the fortuitous dawn of a new kind of interest in American Indian baskets across the country. A craze for authentic Indian things in general began to spread, and basketry made by women drew the most fervent attention—especially from middle- and upper-class white women. Their desire to preserve production and promote consumption of what became considered a precious craft quickly evolved, among many of them, into concern for the very survival of communities they saw in desperate need. Native American women in the South, like their counterparts elsewhere, just as quickly saw an opportunity to ramp up their communities' pursuit of federal protection and recognition. The network of diplomacy resulting from the Chitimachas' relationship with Mary Bradford is one especially important example.[4]

During the first two decades of the twentieth century, the Chitimachas were among the most besieged American Indians in the South. The invasive spread of sugar plantations along Bayou Teche over the nineteenth century had already drastically reduced their territory and diminished their access to resources—including the rivercane still woven into baskets. Through the adaptive forms of livelihood and trade described in chapter 2, they did manage to preserve attachment to places of spiritual as well as material importance. But now the Chitimacha people were confronting a barrage of dangers. Liens on unpayable debt threatened the remains of their land. Several members of the tribe were murdered in two separate encounters with white neighbors, who were also suspected of poisoning the Chitimachas' cisterns. Offscourings from sugar refineries contaminated the bayou, killing its fish and plant life. Chronic respiratory illness also plagued Chitimacha health. And the children lacked access to schools as formal education became more necessary. Amid all of that, Mary McIlhenny Bradford began requesting rivercane baskets and inquiring about their makers.

This interest in basketry woven with rivercane, expressed by an heiress of the plantation South at the dawn of the twentieth century, happened to occur when—after nearly two centuries of encroachment and destruction by the plantation economy—the very source of Chitimacha baskets was near total depletion. Writing to Bradford about her initial request for a basket in 1899, Christine Paul apologized for the time taken to make it and the price now expected for it. It took six weeks of daily work to complete the large double-weave trunk. "If the canes was close to us," she reported, then the price of twenty dollars originally agreed upon would have sufficed. But because an entire week was spent traveling forty miles from home, "way over the grand lake," Paul asked for twenty-five dollars.[5] Canebrakes closer to the Chitimacha community were already destroyed by sugar-cane and cypress-lumber operations, and unprecedented erosion and flooding along the shore of Grand Lake, a sacred space as well as a major source of rivercane, was now rapidly underway. High flooding of the Atchafalaya Basin and Bayou Teche worsened during the early decades of the twentieth century mainly because of water entering it from both the Mississippi and Red Rivers and the federal government's decision not to prevent that flow. For protection of citizens living along the Mississippi below that confluence—especially in the city of New Orleans—the alternative was to build and heighten levees in the basin at the expense of its people's wetland uses and local budgets. Pull-boats dragging timber to shore, fields covered with sugar cane, and even a resort for white beachgoers made matters worse for Indigenous people with rightful claim to fish, hunt, and gather at Grand Lake and surrounding wetlands. And, ironically, all of those operations were also destroying mounds formed with basket-loads of clam shells by generations of Chitimacha men and women to secure the shoreline as well as to hold religious ceremonies.[6]

Despite access to nearby canebrakes becoming more and more difficult, Christine Paul responded immediately and eagerly to Bradford's inquiry about baskets. Access not only to a new market of consumers but also—and more importantly—to a new network of allies outweighed the burden of traveling farther for material. And indeed Bradford, soon to be joined by older sister Sara McIlhenny, quite capably connected Chitimacha weavers with urban merchants and curio dealers, museum curators and ethnologists, and private collectors who proved politically as well as economically beneficial. Christine Paul was a pivotal figure in forming and maintaining that network because of her ability to write as well as weave. During a few years at a nearby Catholic school, she had learned literacy in English well enough to communicate with Bradford and other basket enthusiasts. From her relatives and ancestors, of course, she had learned how to make exquisite Chitimacha baskets. Thanks to some one hundred letters written by Christine Paul, plus many other related documents—discovered a dozen years ago in Mary Bradford's abandoned Avery Island home—we have direct access to a Native American woman's voice that is all too rare for her generation. An example of Indigenous use of literacy to fight back and seek support, Christine Paul's letter-writing diplomacy—perhaps as much as her basket-weaving dexterity—contributed to eventual recognition of the Chitimachas from the U.S. government.[7]

Mary Bradford's principal drive was to encourage survival of what she saw as nearby Indians' creation of authentic and beautiful crafts. Christine Paul's was to channel Bradford's interest not only into monetary income, but into political action. Historians have concentrated on the condescension and commodification that white patrons and consumers brought into such a relationship. Their motives and tastes are treated as the latest phase in a continuum of settler colonialism. But it is now time to pay closer attention to the will and agency of those Native women making the objects. Time to wonder about their purpose and interest in what was often a stressful pace of production and circulation. In the longer span of Indigenous networking and marketing, their work in the early twentieth century was also a phase—but a phase in an ongoing struggle for sovereignty and territory. In other words, Chitimacha and other Native artists continued to strategically navigate non-Native desire for their things—whether it be for their usefulness in daily life, for their value as ethnographic artifacts, or simply for their obvious beauty. Even if the basket fanatics thought they were salvaging objects made by people facing disappearance, the creators of those objects saw themselves engaging in perseverance.[8]

Through her early correspondence with Mary Bradford, mostly over baskets, Christine Paul channeled information about her people's struggles in hope of reaching desperately needed outside assistance. Her relationship with a white woman—across obvious cultural and class lines—could be stressful at times, but had the overall effect of mobilizing Mary and her sister Sara on the tribe's behalf. Bradford's commitment to Chitimacha basketry was bound to draw attention from anthropologists and museum curators, creating an opportunity for her to advance social scientific knowledge at a time when women of her background still had few channels for conveying such expertise (fig. 7). While busily ordering and shipping the baskets and spreading appreciation for them, Bradford closely examined their sizes, shapes, and patterns—modeling her ethnology after that of the curators with whom she corresponded. Orders she sent to Christine Paul included detailed requests for specific types. During a three-year span of her early involvement (November 1901–December 1904), Bradford kept a ledger recording the volume and value of all baskets that passed through her hands. In twenty-six different transactions, nearly 2,000 baskets produced by about fifteen weavers altogether were sold for a total of $2,100. Most of that money reached the Chitimacha women, with Mary keeping $116 of it for prize money, attorney fees, and other miscellaneous expenses.[9]

Obviously Indigenous women were the real source of information that Bradford was gathering and sharing with anthropologists. This role echoed one played two centuries earlier by female ancestors in their relations with natural historians and other colonial interlocutors, like that of the unnamed Chitimacha owned by Le Page du Pratz. Now in the early 1900s, considering threats that confronted them along Bayou Teche, Chitimacha women understood right away that interaction with men like Otis Mason, John Swanton, and Mark Harrington could become another link in an alliance network needed for their community's survival. Scientific attention to the Chitimachas' baskets just might boost appreciation

FIG. 7. Chitimacha baskets on display, 1903, photograph by Mary McIlhenny Bradford. Courtesy of the Avery Island Archives.

for their status as an Indian nation. The influential role played by women—Native and non-Native alike—in facilitating fieldwork undertaken by professional ethnographers during that era has long been overlooked. So Mary Bradford's and Christine Paul's intercultural mediations provide a rare glimpse into both a Native artist's and a local patron's exchange with anthropologists. Both the baskets and letters circulating through those two women's hands illuminate, as Margaret Bruchac has put comparable material, "key moments of intersections, collaboration, and contestation" that contributed to the production of anthropological knowledge.[10]

That same circulation of weavings and writings, however, also contributed to formation of a political network that immediately generated support for tribal interests and eventually influenced reform in Indian policy. From the very beginning of her involvement with Chitimacha basketry, Mary Bradford relied heavily on sustained communication with Neltje Blanchan Doubleday—spouse of publisher Frank Nelson Doubleday and herself a widely read naturalist writer. From her home in New

York City, Doubleday was the single most influential advocate of Native American basketry in the United States, promoting the perpetuation of traditional crafts through her close work with the Women's National Indian Association—an organization that combined philanthropy with advocacy in its attention to Indian affairs.[11] Partnering with Bradford across great distance (the two women apparently never met in person), Doubleday encouraged the Chitimacha weavers through correspondence with Christine Paul and made sure their work reached wealthy collectors, urban stores, national museums, and world fairs. Inspired by Neltje Doubleday's enthusiasm and energy, Mary Bradford worked relentlessly first to feature Chitimacha baskets at the St. Louis world's fair in 1904 and then to place sets produced for the exposition in museums across the country.[12]

Within the larger movement to preserve traditional craftsmanship, baskets made by Native American women drew a degree of fervor approaching fanaticism that lasted from the 1890s into the 1910s. While collecting and displaying baskets in middle- and upper-class homes became a gainful market for what Indigenous women created, contemporary ideas about their handiwork that circulated among many progressive thinkers and activists are likewise not to be overlooked. Updated theories of human development articulated by social scientists, philanthropists, and social workers were now tacking another layer of self-serving rhetoric and imagery onto representation of Indigenous women.[13] And as the nation's most active leader in the campaign to preserve and promote Indigenous basketry, Neltje Doubleday eagerly contributed to that discourse. "While primitive man, of all races, waged war and hunted," she wrote in 1901, "of necessity, primitive woman was ever the constructive element in society, the homemaker, the conserver of industry and thrift, the manufacturer . . . of the raw products of nature into useful and sometimes beautiful forms." This widely held notion of "primitive matriarchy," however, still assigned to men the primary role in economic development. "Where primitive women left off," Doubleday wrote, "civilized men, at a comparatively recent date, were able to take the work from their hands, apply machinery to it and convert the manufacture of textiles into one of the great staples of commerce for the world." She nonetheless preached that "no student of races, of the evolution of art, or folk-lore or of comparative religions can afford to neglect the Indian basket."[14]

While Chitimacha women wove a network of basket diplomacy reaching unforeseen as well as sought-after corners of American society, the McIlhenny sisters dispatched various inquiries into possible means of education for Chitimacha youth being denied admission into white schools by the state of Louisiana. As a result of that effort, more than twenty tribal members attended Carlisle Indian Industrial School between 1906 and 1915. For children and adolescents from Louisiana's bayou country, contact with Indigenous people from across the country as well as with white employers in Carlisle's outwork system certainly expanded their horizon. Some, however, did suffer illness and even death all too prevalent in many Indian boarding schools.[15]

While Chitimacha youth were attending Carlisle, the curriculum at Indian schools happened to be undergoing a notable shift in purpose: from total de-Indianization to selective encouragement of Indian arts and crafts. Hampton Institute began enrolling Indigenous pupils before the founding of Carlisle, and one of those students—a Cherokee woman from western North Carolina—made sure that its studio class featured southern rivercane basketry. After graduating from Hampton in 1899, Arizona Swayney returned to her community to learn "from some of the old Indian women those secrets of their art which are in danger of being lost." She was then hired by her alma mater to teach basketry and pottery, demonstrating her own skill as a creator of Cherokee double-woven baskets.[16] At Carlisle, during the time of Chitimacha enrollment there, arts and crafts were also being taught by a Native American woman. Angel De Cora of the Ho-Chunk nation was a formally trained artist and illustrator who not only advanced arts and crafts curriculum at Carlisle, but played an instrumental role in encouraging school officials and teachers across the United States to recognize the economic potential as well as the aesthetic value of Indigenous material culture, especially baskets, textiles, and beadwork. That ascendant sentiment favoring protection and promotion of Native arts and crafts would eventually culminate in major reform of Indian policy by the 1930s. It also merged with a transformation underway in the wider art world, where modern artists, art critics, anthropologists, along with art-and-design educators—driven in part by nationalist and primitivist notions—began seeing what had long been considered artifacts and crafts as works of art. The high regard and widespread recognition earned by Chitimacha weavers over the preceding decades found a lasting place in the world of Native American art.[17]

Of more immediate importance back home, however, Chitimacha women were wisely turning their children's enrollment at Carlisle into another link in their chain of basket diplomacy. Although those pupils from a small community in south Louisiana might be easy to overlook in the much wider and painful record of Indian boarding schools, their relatively brief encounter with the system mattered a great deal to the Chitimachas. In a Jim Crow South insisting they could only attend schools for African American children, the very presence of Chitimachas in the federal government's largest Indian boarding school accentuated their people's Indianness at a critical moment. Not surprisingly, several of the students enrolled at Carlisle were either children of weavers or weavers themselves. And as one of the pupils experienced in making rivercane baskets, Pauline Paul—Christine Paul's sister-in-law—swiftly mobilized her personal link to Carlisle in her community's ongoing battle for survival. "There are white people here," Pauline wrote to the school's superintendent Moses Friedman after returning home, who are trying to take "our last pice of land" and saying "we not Indian." Friedman, of course, had to know that Pauline's people are Indian by virtue of their enrollment in the government's boarding school. Other Indians in the United States "have there rights," Paul declared, so "we don't see how Congress don't do some thing for us." While she was pleading with the head of Carlisle to communicate with Congress on behalf of the Chitimachas, her cousin Mamie Vilcan—still enrolled at the boarding school in Pennsylvania—appealed from Carlisle directly to the U.S. Commissioner of Indian Affairs. Having received word from her people in Charenton, "asking me to write you a letter concerning land affairs," Mamie wondered if he "would help the Indians" against the "taking and selling" of their land. "Your kindness will be greatly appreciated," she wrote.[18]

The Chitimachas, indeed, were facing the greatest threat yet to their survival when one neighboring sugar-cane planter demanded seizure and sale of their remaining land for default of a debt. Relying heavily on a network woven with baskets, the community and its McIlhenny allies desperately pursued any assistance that might preempt a foreclosure auction. Links with anthropologists, with Carlisle and other federal officials, and with national organizations were quickly mobilized with requests for intervention. In the thick of this mobilization, Delphine Stouff—a skilled Chitimacha basket maker—was certain about the federal government's authority and responsibility to protect Indian lands against alienation, but frustrated by its indifference. So now she wrote a direct appeal to anthropologist Mark Harrington, who had visited the Chitimachas in 1908. Although "some said we not Indians," she thought that Harrington could prove otherwise. "You know yourself you come here and borth [bought] old thing we had made by my parents." Hoping the anthropologist could appeal to Congress on her people's behalf, Stouff declared that "we are Indian too" and thus deserved "the same right like orther Indians."[19] Harrington, supporting the political agency ascribed by Stouff to Chitimacha material culture, forwarded her letter to his Seneca Indian friend Arthur Parker. Secretary of the newly organized Society of American Indians, as well as an archaeologist and ethnologist at New York's state museum, Parker then sent his own appeal to the commissioner of Indian affairs. He also published in the society's journal Harrington's account of the 1901 and 1908 Chitimacha murders. Despite that surge in basket diplomacy, however, government intervention was not forthcoming in time. It took, instead, a last-minute loan from Sara McIlhenny in 1914 to pay the debt, halt seizure, and save the land. Two years later, the U.S. Congress reimbursed McIlhenny and established federal trust over the land, finally securing tribal possession for the Chitimachas.[20]

Although exceptionally transparent because of documentation saved by Mary Bradford, the political mobilization of basketry by Chitimacha women was by no means unique in the South. Comparable evidence for the Cherokees in western North Carolina has been skillfully explored by Sarah Hill and for the Coushattas in southwest Louisiana by Denise Bates, Linda Langley, and Jay Precht.[21] And in both Mississippi and Louisiana during the early twentieth century, Choctaw people also engaged in basket diplomacy in pursuit of protection against corrosive forces. Those still living near Bayou Lacombe and lower Pearl River, as discussed in chapter 2, had counted on Father Adrien Rouquette for much-needed security and support during the midcentury's turbulent years. And still in need of allies after the priest's death in 1887, Choctaw communities along Mississippi's Gulf Coast as well as Lake Pontchartrain fortunately managed to find new ones in a timely way—largely because the period's craze over Indian baskets had spread among several influential white women in and around New Orleans, where seasonally the McIlhenny sisters also spent a good bit of their time. And the high visibility of rivercane basketry made by Choctaw people that would draw their attention is reflected in the 1890 census summary of Indians still living in Mississippi. Among various items they sold in that state's larger towns every spring, as noted in the report, were "baskets made in considerable numbers from the cane." It further remarked that "white boys in the towns at the season are generally supplied with blowguns, made by these Indians from the hollow cane stems, and furnished with darts fitted with feathers or cotton down."[22]

While visiting New Orleans in 1901 to examine the archaeological collection of the late Dr. Joseph Jones, Stewart Culin learned that Choctaw people from the north shore of Lake Pontchartrain still spent Sundays in the New Orleans French Market selling baskets and gumbo filé. Consequently, this curator-collector from the University of Pennsylvania's science museum took a steamer across the lake to carry out some impromptu fieldwork among Choctaws living near Mandeville. "At the first hut I found several men and women seated about their little cabin, the women plaiting baskets from strips of split cane." "At first, listless and indifferent," as described in his report, "they soon became interested and animated, answered my inquiries freely and permitted me to photograph them." Culin also noted that these Choctaws grew yams and corn around their homes, earned wages doing odd jobs, and made baskets and ground sassafras for sale. And for marketing their products in New Orleans, they were accorded "free transportation across the lake." When Culin inquired about "objects of their manufacture, they brought out ornamental baskets, *ta-po shek*, and long cane blow guns, *ka-tshun-pa*, with darts, *shoma-tai*, which they make for sale." He "also found flat winnowing baskets, *off-ko*, and large carrying baskets, *kehshe*, made of split cane, and in one of the houses, a rude fiddle, *tsle-po-shet*, consisting of a joint of cane, with four strings."

Culin also sighted "a pair of old rackets, *ka-bu-cha*" precisely matching those used in a game of stickball that he had witnessed being played by teams of "French-speaking negroes" in New Orleans. This man who would later be called "Old Things" by Zuni people in New Mexico because of his notorious methods of collecting cultural objects did manage, "with much difficulty" as he put it, to acquire one of those ball-game sticks. According to the Penn Museum's accession records, all of the Choctaw things assembled by Culin were likely displayed at the Pan-American exposition in Buffalo, New York. And though the real-life burdens confronted by Choctaw and other Indigenous women in the Jim Crow South were apparently of little concern to ethnologists like Stewart Culin, that rather large and uniquely crafted burden basket he purchased on the north shore of Lake Pontchartrain must have caused some faraway fairgoers and museum visitors to at least wonder for a moment about its maker.[23]

Living nearer to Choctaw basket makers and knowing them better was Josephine Ellis, widow of Louisiana politician E. John Ellis and founding chair of the New Orleans chapter of the Women's National Indian Association (WNIA). Ellis was the woman responsible for initiating communication between Neltje Doubleday and Mary Bradford that proved invaluable to the Chitimachas' basket diplomacy. The Crescent City chapter of the WNIA, whose membership stood at about fifty by the end of the nineteenth century, met monthly at the Christian Women's Exchange on Lafayette Square, where Louisiana Indian baskets among other crafts made by rural women were readily available for purchase. As southern vice-president of the national association for two decades (until her death in 1912), Ellis was able to inform a nationwide audience about the particular circumstances faced by Louisiana and Mississippi communities.[24] From her summer home near Amite, Josephine Ellis developed a vigorous patronage relationship with Choctaw weavers on Lake Pontchartrain's north shore, and—resembling the McIlhenny sisters in their relationship with the Chitimachas—she helped their baskets reach distant expositions, museums, and stores. Ellis also regularly assembled money and goods from fellow WNIA members for Indian groups as far away as California as well as for local Choctaws. In 1898 she facilitated placement of a troubled Choctaw girl named Lilestan in the Poydras Female Orphan Asylum and continued to support her education—which led to that girl becoming a Christian missionary to other Choctaws.[25]

At a New Orleans chapter meeting of the Women's National Indian Association in April 1901, Josephine Ellis told the ladies in attendance that "Indians should be encouraged in the art and industry of basket-making, which is getting to be a lost art." Considering how thousands of "inferior baskets are brought over yearly from Germany," she wondered what establishment of the enterprise among American Indians, "said to be the most expert basket weavers in the world," would "mean to the race."[26] By 1908 the National Indian Association's annual report announced that the New Orleans branch, besides engaging in the organization's general work, "has been interested during the past year chiefly among the basket-maker Chetamachans of Louisiana . . . as well as in the Choctaws of . . . Mississippi." And for the following year's national meeting in New York, Josephine Ellis even sent a letter reporting that "our little band of Chemanche near Avery's Island, in southern Louisiana, are now self-supporting with their artistic basket-work."[27]

Eliza Nicholson—the *New Orleans Daily Picayune* owner, editor, and writer busy with a range of public causes—also circulated Louisiana Indian basketry to distant collectors. Having grown up in the piney woods of south Mississippi knowing Choctaw neighbors, Nicholson became an influential literary advocate for their basketry.[28] In published articles and private correspondence, she vividly described how Choctaw women turned "the thinnest shavings of cane" with "the subtly sweet odor" of springtime woods into "deliciously odd shapes" that showed "contempt for all the laws of curves and angles." Nicholson was responsible for many Louisiana Indian baskets appearing for display and purchase at the 1893 world's fair in Chicago, as Mary Bradford would be for the St. Louis exposition a decade later. And she used her professional ties with fellow journalists in Europe as well as in the United States to make sure Choctaw baskets reached their homes. Thanking Nicholson for the gift of what was most likely a burden basket, Mary L. Booth, editor of *Harper's Bazaar,* called it "the most unique thing I ever saw," placed it in her library's "cozy corner," and reported that "all who have seen it marvel at its quaint shape and pattern." "Those Indians of yours at Bay St. Louis," she exclaimed, "are real artists." Never in Nicholson's articles and correspondence did she identify by name the female artists actually producing such objects, and the few personal glimpses that do show up reflected—in her own words—"the romantic association that must always cling to the fast disappearing Indian race." "Sometimes there comes to the gate of our Bay St. Louis home with Indian baskets to sell," she wrote in 1890, "a pretty nineteenth century Pocahontas," causing one to "wonder by what strange intuition she learned to make so many baskets." The agency of Indigenous women remains consistently veiled by use of such language.[29]

Hired by Eliza Nicholson as a full-time reporter and the first woman to work on the *Daily Picayune* staff, Martha Field published early in her time there a lengthy and vivid account of the Choctaws living at Bayou La Croix. Located fifteen miles back of Bay St. Louis and numbering about sixty people, this community centered itself around a Roman Catholic church and marketed foods, medicines, and handicrafts in Mississippi Gulf Coastal towns. When Field asked if there were any baskets for sale, "Mrs. Bilbo," the chief's wife, handed her a few made of rivercane woven into different shapes—heart, elbow, and wall pocket. The journalist regretted having to report, however, that these Choctaws were now making fewer baskets because destruction of or loss of access to nearby canebrakes required them to travel farther to harvest the material.[30] Although seldom mentioning Indians in later travel reports, Field did refer in a couple of her writings to Choctaw women selling their wares in the New Orleans French Market. One column published in 1888 offered an imaginative glimpse into how uptown New Orleans women at that time were beginning to venture more freely across town and thereby taking greater interest in the Vieux Carré. Two residents of uptown's Garden District stayed for a week in the city's downtown "French Town," bringing easels, brushes, and pencils with them. Every morning, between stopping at the Morning Star coffee stall and then proceeding to other Vieux Carré sights, these ladies would look over "the baskets, big and little, of the Choctaw women squatting on the stones in the market court."[31]

Attracted to baskets made by Choctaw women living near Florenville, Louisiana—her home north of Lake Pontchartrain—New Orleans artist Cora Bremer became a very active promoter of their production and circulation. In 1907 she wrote and distributed a privately printed pamphlet detailing at great length what life was like for Choctaw Indians around Pearl River and how their rivercane baskets were created. "Basket making," Bremer believed, "is a natural art among the women of this tribe." And she purposefully chose the word art rather than craft to characterize work "intended for use in the most humble and utilitarian sense, of a cunningness of technique, a striving to express grace of line, geometric exactness and warmth of color, which is the proof, the foundation of art."[32] Thanks to Cora Bremer's correspondence with Mary Bradford during the year 1902, we catch a rare look inside her interaction with specific Choctaw weavers. To encourage maintenance of quality and authenticity in their work, Bremer sought advice from Bradford in regard to issuing prizes, establishing prices, and finding buyers. The two patrons of local Indian basketry also requested from each other particular types of baskets for inclusion in their own collections and for filling orders from their respective correspondents. In one exchange, Bremer acquired for Bradford a large Choctaw pack basket made with only natural dyes. She was "compelled" by Felicie, the weaver, "to give her the sum of $5.50 for it," so after "adding the cost of transportation from the swamps to N.O.," it would require a total of six dollars from Mary.[33]

Again like Mary Bradford, Cora Bremer was eager to promote the visibility of local Indians among anthropologists as well as commercial buyers. When gathering a collection of Choctaw objects for New York City's American Museum of Natural History in 1902, Bremer reported to Franz Boas the "effort" and "diplomacy" it demanded. The greatest expenditure went into acquiring from "Old Joe" or Chief "Little Bird" deep in the swamps a dugout canoe, a silver crown, and some beaded sashes. In contrast with those "relics," she wrote, baskets representing different styles and valued at eighteen dollars were "not difficult to procure—as I can get them near our place in the country."[34] In later years, Bremer donated several Choctaw baskets to Louisiana's State Museum in New Orleans and helped organize its American Indian exhibit. While museum curators and visitors likely considered all Indigenous objects to be cultural artifacts, for the people who produced and sold them they were much more—sources of income, sure, but also tools of diplomacy.[35]

Although the federal government removed many Louisiana Choctaws to the Choctaw Nation in Oklahoma under pressure to enroll in 1902–1903—"sixty five of my Choctaw left here for Indian Territory last week," Bremer lamented to Bradford—a small community of stalwarts did stay in St. Tammany Parish.[36] Several years later, they became the source of information and material culture for Smithsonian anthropologist David Bushnell's fieldwork at Bayou Lacombe. Although Bushnell thought their basketry "greatly inferior to that of a generation ago," he nonetheless called those Choctaw women on the north shore of Lake Pontchartrain "excellent basket makers." Considering their best baskets to be those made of cane, the anthropologist included in his published report two photographs featuring the style he thought most interesting, a pack basket or *kish'e* made by Pisatuntema, also known as Emma (figs. 8–9). Daughter of a previous headman and baptized as a child by Father Rouquette, Pisatuntema was now the oldest member of the community and a principal source of Bushnell's ethnological information (fig. 10). The weavers were currently using palmetto stems to make basketry because, as Bushnell learned, "cane is no longer found near-by, and to obtain it a journey has to be made to Pearl river, some fifteen or twenty miles away." Nonetheless, as he also noted, the Choctaws were still exchanging "large numbers of small baskets provided with handles" for various goods in the stores of nearby towns. "These are purchased by strangers," he added, "and taken away as examples of native art."[37]

David Bushnell himself always made sure to "take away" baskets among other cultural objects from whatever Indigenous community he visited. Like so many ethnologists and archaeologists of his generation eager to build collections for themselves as well as for institutions, Bushnell acquired an inordinate quantity of cultural objects from the people he studied in the Lower Mississippi Valley and other parts of the South. In 1917, while still on the Smithsonian Institution's payroll, Bushnell sold to the American Museum of Natural History in New York—for five hundred dollars—a hundred Choctaw, Chitimacha, Atakapa, and Alabama baskets

FIG. 8. *Choctaw Woman Carrying Basket on Back,* 1909, photograph by David I. Bushnell. National Anthropological Archives, Smithsonian Institution, BAE GN 01102B22.

FIG. 9. *Choctaw Boy in Pack Basket,* 1909,
photograph by David I. Bushnell. National Anthropological Archives,
Smithsonian Institution, BAE GN 01102B16b.

FIG. 10. *Pisatuntema (Emma)* (Choctaw), 1909, photograph by David I. Bushnell. National Anthropological Archives, Smithsonian Institution, BAE GN 01102B20.

that he had assembled during his travels to Louisiana. "I know it would be impossible to duplicate some of the specimens," he told curator Clark Wissler. Bushnell learned that the Atakapa baskets were made before 1850 "from the old lady from whom I obtained them, not an Indian, but a member of one of the old families of New Orleans." One basket "made by an Alibamu woman living in St. Landry parish Louisiana," according to Bushnell, dated to "about the year 1870."[38]

Preoccupation with the oldest basketry in part reflected an all too common belief held by anthropologists and other collectors that Native American arts, if not Native Americans as a people, were inexorably headed for extinction. A year after his sale of baskets to the New York museum, David Bushnell presented a paper to the Louisiana Historical Association summarizing "the manners and customs" of St. Tammany Parish Choctaws. At that meeting in New Orleans, he encouraged others "to become interested in preserving notes on the Indians scattered throughout Louisiana." Why? Because "some may represent the last of a little-known tribe, and may possess knowledge of inestimable value to the historian and ethnologist." In "another generation," Bushnell concluded, "little will remain." No mention was made, of course, to the discreet diplomacy that Native women were still deploying in the production and circulation of their basketry.[39]

Among the more populous Choctaw communities still in east-central Mississippi, numbering more than a thousand people, the government's final closing of the Oklahoma Choctaw tribal roll now threatened them more than ever with disappearance since they refused to depart. For them as well, though, basket enthusiasts became helpful allies at a moment of intense pressure. Married to a lumber businessman and living in Laurel, Mississippi, Catherine Marshall Gardiner was without any doubt the Gulf South's most serious collector of Native American basketry. At the start of the twentieth century, she began aggressively assembling hundreds of baskets mostly through correspondence with dealers, museum curators, other private collectors, and government agents and school supervisors on Indian reservations. Although already an admirer of Indian baskets, Gardiner knew little about them and even less about how to find them until reading in a newspaper that North American Indian basketry "would become scarce for the reason that the younger squaws with opportunity for education and with opportunity to purchase domestic utensils and ornaments would no longer make the necessary sacrifices in gathering material nor use their time for the laborious weaving." So she decided to assemble a collection before it became too late. In 1923 Gardiner donated her entire collection to the Lauren Rogers Museum of Art in Laurel, one of today's finest places to view Indigenous baskets from across North America.[40]

While receiving baskets of all kinds from distant sources, Gardiner also bought rivercane and white oak baskets directly from nearby Choctaw weavers as well as from local stores, making sure that they reached museums and private collectors around the country. One collector in Bridgeport, Connecticut, seeing Gardiner's name mentioned in Otis Mason's popular book on Indian basketry, began requesting Louisiana and Mississippi Indian baskets from her. When Gardiner purchased in-person a rivercane burden basket from an unnamed Choctaw woman in Heidelberg, the seller—as recorded in her meticulous notes—"refused to part with the much worn carrying strap; neither a new one nor money to buy several new ones tempted her, her answer always being 'You take your money and buy you a new one.'"[41]

While their baskets were gaining attention from collectors, the Choctaws' desire to remain in their Mississippi homeland also grabbed notice from various directions. In contrast with Louisiana politicians, Mississippi's congressional delegation aggressively advocated for Choctaws in that state to recover the tribal status lost and receive the land allotments promised in the Treaty of Dancing Rabbit Creek. As Katherine Osburn has persuasively argued, that support was mainly driven by white Mississippi leaders' ideological association of the Confederacy's lost cause in the Civil War with treatment suffered by the Choctaws at the hands of the federal government before that war. Of course, as she shows, this benevolence overlooked the role played by white Mississippians in driving the Choctaw nation out of the state and also assumed that those Choctaw people still living in Mississippi would eventually vanish.[42]

In the Mississippi Choctaws' pursuit of tribal status and land ownership, several outsiders promising to file petitions for them proved to be untrustworthy. Among only a few earnest allies, however, were Baptist minister and hotel owner James E. Arnold and his wife. Up against stubborn insistence by the Office of Indian Affairs that no Choctaw nation other than that in Oklahoma existed, Arnold testified on the Mississippi Choctaws' behalf before the House Committee on Indian Affairs. Both of the Arnolds, meanwhile, were promoting and selling Choctaw baskets across the country. "Since time memorial," Mrs. Arnold wrote in one letter, "the Choctaw Indians have lived in Mississippi, and have made baskets of the reed cane which grows in the swamps of the south." "Works of art" that "combine beauty with long wearing qualities and light weight," she proclaimed, "there are no finer baskets made, and nothing nicer for Christmas presents." When the Arnolds moved to Washington DC during the 1920s to continue lobbying, the cellar of their new home became—as reported in a lengthy *Washington Post* story—"the distributing center" for Choctaw basketry. From there, apparently hundreds of baskets were being circulated among church groups, schools, and women's clubs for sale. For the Choctaw women weaving them back in Mississippi, those baskets served the obvious purpose of political action. Allocation of special funds and establishment of an Indian Office agency were already in the works, resulting eventually with formal recognition of today's Mississippi Band of Choctaw Indians.[43]

For several different nations in this part of the South, production of basketry for the arts and crafts market was one means of performing Indianness at a dire moment in time. Indigenous Studies scholars in general now recognize how, in the face of assimilationist pressures, performance of Indian identity became ever more essential, whether it be staged, crafted, or written. But playing to the dominant society's expectations—even in pursuit of maintaining sovereignty and territory—did not come without tension and even risk. Although not directly subjected to forms of assimilationism imposed on Indians elsewhere in the United States because the federal government refused to even notice them, Indians in the Jim Crow South nonetheless confronted an existential threat to their identity and status. Virginia's Racial Purity Act of 1924, drafted by that state's white supremacist registrar of vital statistics, is the best-known example of how Native Americans and people of mixed ancestry were reclassified into either Whites or Blacks.[44]

In the state of Louisiana, Houma people's efforts to enroll their children in public schools were blocked by a superintendent who throughout his reign of forty years (1914–55) insisted that they were not American Indians. When H. L. Billiot initiated a case in state court to overcome that official's refusal to admit his three sons, he confronted virulent charges of having some degree of African ancestry. Across the Jim Crow South, school systems operated as a front line of racialization. Claiming to have white relatives and even denying any relationship with Black neighbors—as Billiot did—would not matter in an education system divided only into White and Black schools. A white supremacist like the Terrebonne Parish superintendent saw Houma families wanting their children to attend "White schools," obviously much better funded than "Negro schools," as people trying to break through the wall of racial segregation. The "free people of color" category inherited from centuries of slavery was re-weaponized against southern Indian communities, with Houmas in south Louisiana now being called 'Sabines," Lumbees in eastern North Carolina called "Croatans," and Choctaws in south Alabama called "Cajuns"—monikers that implied mixture with African Americans. Lacking recognition as American Indians by the federal government, the only chance for Houmas to gain access to a decent education—until segregation of public education became illegal—came in schools operated by religious organizations. In their ongoing battle for the right to represent themselves as an Indigenous nation, they would by the 1930s also find useful allies through their production of baskets and other crafts.[45]

Insistence upon a binary system of racial separation had the effect of burying whatever degree of ambiguity and fluidity actually existed among many different groups of people—whether, for example, they be Sicilian immigrants or creoles of color in the Gulf South.[46] But for Indigenous people wanting to preserve their autonomy, racialization had political as well as social consequence. While African Americans sought equal inclusion in the political body of the United States, American Indians sought protected separation from it. Any pursuit of Indian rights, in what Barbara

Fields has called the minefield of racecraft, required emboldening boundaries with other southerners, especially with Black southerners.[47] Consequently, demonstration of separateness through material culture or some other cultural form might matter for recovery of land and recognition. Basketry, which for previous centuries had already been woven by Native American women into a versatile representation of belonging and identity, did just that.[48]

CONCLUSION

Recognition of the Chitimacha Tribe of Louisiana and of the Mississippi Band of Choctaw Indians by the third decade of the twentieth century marked the start of steady acknowledgment by state and federal governments of other Indigenous nations in this and other regions of the American South. This has been, and continues to be, a process nonetheless fraught with all too predictable obstacles, conflicts, and setbacks. As Angela Gonzales, Judy Kertész, and Gabrielle Tayac have emphasized, countering racialized constructions of identity reinforced by early twentieth-century eugenics proved nearly insurmountable for many communities that had nonetheless preserved their all-important tribal identity.[1] And even when the grip of Jim Crow rule began to loosen, denial of recognition to many southern groups persisted largely because of non-Native apprehension of consequential claims to Native lands and resources unlawfully taken over the centuries. Some southern states, however, did respond to Indian initiatives by formalizing and facilitating relations with tribal governments.[2]

In Louisiana today eleven groups are now recognized by the state, and four by the federal government. The state-recognized category includes, among several other groups, the United Houma Nation, the Choctaw-Apache Tribe of Ebarb, the Isle de Jean Charles Band of Biloxi Chitimacha Confederation of Muskogees, and the Clifton Choctaw Tribe of Louisiana. Federally recognized are the Chitimacha Tribe of Louisiana (1916), the Coushatta Tribe of Louisiana (1973), the Tunica-Biloxi Tribe of Louisiana (1981), and the Jena Band of Choctaw (1995). Over in Mississippi there is the Mississippi Band of Choctaw Indians and in Alabama the Poarch Band of Creek Indians (1984). The Alabama-state-recognized MOWA Band of

Choctaw Indians, like Louisiana's Houma nation, have been seeking federal recognition for quite a while. Among all of these nations and across the South, women have risen in number as tribal leaders.[3]

The role of basketry among these Indigenous communities took different paths over the last century or so, continuing and even expanding as a craft among some but persisting as an important expression of identity and tradition among nearly all of them. Cherokees in North Carolina and Choctaws in Mississippi, the most populous groups among southern weavers, have carried on rivercane basketry with remarkable versatility. And though the Chitimachas today count only a few cane-basket weavers, restoration of the Chitimacha language currently underway is closely tied to the tribe's basket-making tradition and history. The Poarch Creek Nation in south Alabama as well as the Chitimachas, Cherokees, and Choctaws have developed rivercane projects, planting and maintaining canebrakes that enhance their reservation environments and ensure future harvesting for basketry. In a region where less than 5 percent of a plant once so prolific still exists, this Native American initiative is extremely important for wider recovery of the South's environmental health.[4]

In addition to contemporary weavers within the communities, some prominent Native American artists have taken rivercane work in noteworthy directions. Norma Howard, member of the Choctaw Nation of Oklahoma, uses thousands of individual basket-weave strokes to create scenes of everyday life with tempera on paper. Choctaw women weaving and using cane baskets are depicted in many of her paintings. Sarah Sense, growing up in California, learned about rivercane basketry from her Chitimacha grandfather and Choctaw grandmother. Using mixed media with photography, she weaves images and ancestral designs into a wide range of subjects (plate 6). Her work offers historical and environmental commentary spanning continents and oceans. Shan Goshorn of the Eastern Band of Cherokee Indians is perhaps the weaver best known for creation of basketry that expresses political and social activism. Before her untimely death in 2018, Goshorn cut watercolor papers and photographic prints into narrow strips to weave into familiar forms of Cherokee basketry, with words and images appearing outside and inside to record historical experiences (plate 7). Carol Emarthle-Douglas, an artist of Seminole and Northern Arapaho descent, has produced a prize-winning basket that closely captures the theme of this book (plate 8). Although not a direct reference to rivercane basketry, *Cultural Burdens* features miniature back-pack baskets held by a total of twenty-two silhouettes woven both inside and outside the main basket. The miniatures represent styles of burden baskets made by different tribes, including Cherokee and Seminole. This work, as explained by Emarthle-Douglas, "celebrates women and all that they have contributed to our culture, past and present." Altogether, these artists are engaged in what Tuscarora artist and scholar Jolene Rickard calls "the deployment of tradition as strategic cultural resistance," asserting Native sovereignty and identity through twenty-first-century visualizations of traditional material culture.[5]

Basket diplomacy for certain remains a vital part of southern Indian sovereignty and identity, so let me end with a couple of recent examples from the Lower Mississippi Valley. When in 2016 the U.S. Secretary of the Interior invited the Chitimacha Tribe of Louisiana to send two children to First Lady Michelle Obama's "Let's Move" event at the White House, cultural director Kimberly Walden escorted two fifth-grade girls to Washington. The two students from the Chitimacha Tribal School and their chaperon met both the President and First Lady, participated in harvesting the White House Garden and making vegetable pizza, and visited several museums, monuments, and memorials in the capital city. They were also treated to a private tour of the Smithsonian Institution's collection of Chitimacha things: tools, weapons, clothing, but mostly baskets—just one example of how Native Americans are currently reconnecting with basketry and other cultural objects held in museums around the country. The following year, a delegation from Isle de Jean Charles, the Biloxi-Chitimacha-Choctaw community now undergoing relocation from the Louisiana coast as "climate-change refugees," spent time at the Smithsonian to examine that museum's stored collection of Chitimacha baskets. As reported in the *New Orleans Times-Picayune,* "they were looking for evidence to supplement their petition for official 'acknowledgement' from the federal government." This visit was part of a community research program called "Recovering Voices."[6]

A few years ago, the Frist Museum of Art in Nashville was planning to host an exhibition called "Hearts of Our People" from late September 2019 to mid-January 2020. That exhibit, originating at the Minneapolis Institute of Art, would feature more than a hundred works created by Native American women from ancient times to the present. Among the objects appearing in "Hearts of Our People"—to my great delight—was a set of double-woven and intricately patterned baskets made more than a century ago by Chitimacha weaver Clara Darden, a woman who was crucial to the start of how her community mobilized material objects for political as well as cultural survival.[7] That set, not incidentally, once belonged to the provost of the University of Pennsylvania—Dr. William Pepper—who was responsible for sponsoring E. A. "Ned" McIlhenny's famous ethnographic and natural history expedition to Alaska in 1897. So no doubt, his sisters' Chitimacha work is responsible for those baskets reaching Philadelphia.[8] As someone already familiar with museum staff at the Frist, I asked them to include in the programming of events Melissa Darden—a descendant of Clara Darden and a weaver herself who furthermore currently chairs the Chitimacha Tribe of Louisiana. Darden graciously agreed to travel to middle Tennessee from her home in south Louisiana and participate in "Hearts of Our People." On a busy Sunday at the museum, she demonstrated her artistry and explained its cultural and historical context for visitors. Additional time that she spent walking with me through the entire exhibition and updating her on my own work proved to be particularly beneficial for me. With Clara Darden's beautiful creations displayed in a case before us, Melissa Darden's personal and enthusiastic explanation of the patterns woven into the Chitimacha baskets represented another form of basket diplomacy.

Like the subterranean chain roots, or rhizomes, of the rivercane plant itself—and like the resourceful networks that Native American women created with that plant over the generations covered in this volume—it has always been about remaining connected to the land and to each other. Millennia of Native Americans' lived experiences in specific geographical locations, as one team of historians recently wrote, "underscore the importance of recognizing Indigenous sovereignty as intimately interwoven with *place* and profoundly accountable to the more-than-human kin who comprise the entire network of relations: animals, plants, waterways, and the earth."[9] In the Lower Mississippi Valley and elsewhere in the American South, generations of seasonal travel for work and trade—a somewhat inconspicuous and selective form of interaction with colonizers—did not loosen Native attachment to the homeland or weaken determination to retain or recover sovereignty over parts of it. Although Native Americans in the South generally seemed absent or absorbed in the eyes of U.S. citizens and officials, they in fact had never abandoned their own struggles for political and cultural autonomy.

As many well know, there is a widespread tradition in the South of claiming descent from a "Cherokee Princess." Over 40 percent of respondents polled three decades ago by the University of North Carolina's Institute for Research in Social Science thought they had an Indian ancestor, indicating that southerners were more likely to claim descent from American Indians than from Confederate soldiers.[10] Like the Pocahontas myth, such claims tend to relegate Native women to the role of "handmaidens" who essentially were handing themselves and their people's land over to colonizing men. Conflating women's bodies with the land became in essence a means of denying complicity in acts of conquest. The persistence of this fantasy's dismissive effect is evidenced by a recent U.S. president's habitual slinging of the Pocahontas slur against a political opponent and, more importantly, the horrific number of Indigenous women and girls who are missing and murdered. Whether stereotyped as either "the hot-blooded Indian princess" or "the Indian squaw plodding behind her man," as Clara Sue Kidwell stated the matter, Indian women "are not real people."[11]

In this book I have attempted something of a counternarrative to a racialized and sexualized misrepresentation that for too long has concealed the real complexity of Indigenous women's roles in Indian and white contact. Faced with the shattering impacts of early colonial violence on their families and communities, American Indian women in the early South contributed significantly to alliance and trade with colonial people for the survival of their own people. Then, as dispossession accelerated and intensified in the plantation South, they adapted work, movement, and exchange in order to remain connected to their territory—to its spiritual as well as material resources. And by the twentieth century, Native American women in the Jim Crow South effectively turned cultural objects woven from such resources into instruments of political action on behalf of Native sovereignty and territory.

ACKNOWLEDGMENTS

I will always be grateful for the invitation bestowed upon me by Louisiana State University's Department of History to deliver the Walter Lynwood Fleming Lectures. It provided me with the opportunity not only to share in a public forum some of my thoughts centering on southern history, but to spend time with colleagues and friends in that department. Knowing Alecia Long, Paul Hoffman, and Kodi Roberts beforehand, I am particularly grateful to them for their attention and encouragement during the visit. Gaines Foster and Mary Mikell hosted a wonderful reception at their home, which I enjoyed and appreciated very much. Through advanced arrangements and desperately needed assistance at the lectern, Leslie Tuttle made it possible for my talks to reach via live broadcast a wider community of history teachers. I owe thanks to Christine Kooi, the department's chair, and Darlene Albritton, its administrative coordinator, for the careful planning that made sure my travel and stay would go smoothly.

The Fleming Lectures became a much welcome chance for me to test before a diverse audience findings and interpretations already taking shape through my work-in-progress on the Chitimacha Tribe of Louisiana. For invaluable guidance on that manuscript, I owe special thanks to Theda Perdue, Claudio Saunt, and Kimberly Walden. In preparing my Fleming Lectures, I decided to focus on historiographic and thematic topics featuring Indigenous women across a wider part of the South and longer span of time. The chapters for this book, resulting from my expansion of those lectures, then benefited immeasurably from close readings by Peter Wood, Dayna Bowker Lee, and Elizabeth Ellis. I cannot thank them enough for all the insights and suggestions they so generously offered. Additional feedback and advice provided through the press from an anonymous reader was also helpful and appreciated.

My research for this work received plenty of assistance from archival staff at the American Philosophical Society, the American Museum of Natural History's Division of Anthropological Archives, the Historic New Orleans Collection, the Huntington Library, the Lauren Rogers Museum of Art, Louisiana State University's Louisiana and Lower Mississippi Valley Collection, the McIlhenny Company and Avery Island, Inc., Archives, the National Archives, and Tulane University's Louisiana Research Collection. Funds drawn from Vanderbilt University's Holland N. McTyeire Endowment covered the costs of travel to those widespread archives plus the partial cost for production of this book's illustrations. To artists Sarah Sense and Carol Emarthle-Douglas, I am grateful for their kind permission to include images illustrating their remarkable work. The time that chairwoman Melissa Darden and cultural director Kimberly Walden have taken from their busy schedules to see me during visits to the Chitimacha reservation is always appreciated. A drive with Kim to her nation's River Cane Project sites made an impression that undoubtedly influenced what I decided to write for my Fleming Lectures.

I owe special thanks to LSU Press editor-in-chief Rand Dotson and managing editor Catherine L. Kadair for attending to this book so carefully throughout the process. Jo Ann Kiser, the copy editor, earned my gratitude for the close and comprehensive care she gave to the manuscript. Finally, none of the steps taken to research for, and to write, this work would be possible without Rhonda Usner. Whether as my companion on journeys through south Mississippi's piney woods and along oak-lined Bayou Teche, or as my in-house editor and critic, her love and encouragement made this book possible. And living through all of the challenges and difficulties presented by the Covid pandemic certainly confirmed how much I need her.

I dedicate this book to two remarkable scholars whose guidance and friendship over the years have meant more to me than I can adequately express. It was of course the academic privilege of my life to be Peter Wood's first Ph.D. student at Duke University, but more importantly it has been quite a thrill to follow the extraordinary work that he continues to produce and that many others subsequently benefiting from his mentorship have produced. Theda Perdue, throughout my own journey as a historian of the Native American South, has been the kindest and most inspirational of kindred travelers. And like Peter, she has rewarded all of us not only with her own superb scholarship but also with that of the countless students who have received her generous mentorship and encouragement.

NOTES

INTRODUCTION

1. "Chetimaches and Their Land Claims," *New Orleans Daily Picayune,* June 11, 1899.

2. Theda Perdue, "The Legacy of Indian Removal," *Journal of Southern History* 78 (February 2012): 3–36, quote from 36. For assessment of scholarship on southern Indian history, see Christina Snyder and Theda Perdue, "The Native South," *Reinterpreting Southern Histories: Essays in Historiography,* ed. Craig Thompson Friend and Lorri Glover (Baton Rouge: Louisiana State University Press, 2020), 415–44. Also see Andrew K. Frank and Kristofer Ray, "Indians as Southerners; Southerners as Indians: Rethinking the History of the Region," *Native South* 10 (2017): vii–xiv. For a concise overview of American Indians in the South, see Christina Snyder, "The South," *The Oxford Handbook of American Indian History,* ed. Frederick E. Hoxie (New York: Oxford University Press, 2016), 315–34.

3. Stephanie M. H. Camp, *Closer to Freedom: Enslaved Women and Everyday Resistance in the Plantation South* (Chapel Hill: University of North Carolina Press, 2004), quote from 3; Thavolia Glymph, *The Women's Fight: The Civil War's Battles for Home, Freedom, and Nation* (Chapel Hill: University of North Carolina Press, 2020); Kelley Fanto Deetz, *Bound to the Fire: How Virginia's Enslaved Cooks Helped Invent American Cuisine* (Lexington: University Press of Kentucky, 2017); Rebecca Sharpless, *Cooking in Other Women's Kitchens: Domestic Workers in the South, 1865–1960* (Chapel Hill: University of North Carolina Press, 2010). In their recent historiographical essay on gender and sexuality in the Old South, Catherine Clinton and Emily West observe that scholars have only begun to include Native women in the scholarship: Clinton and West, "Gender and Sexuality in the Old South," *Reinterpreting Southern Histories,* 139–65.

4. Rebecca Kugel and Lucy Eldersveld Murphy, eds., *Native Women's History in Eastern North America before 1900: A Guide to Research and Writing* (Lincoln: University of Nebraska Press, 2007), quote from xv; Michelle LeMaster, "Pocahontas Doesn't Live Here Anymore: Women and Gender in the Native South before Removal," *Native South* 7 (2014): 1–32.

5. Brooke M. Bauer, *Becoming Catawba: Catawba Indian Women and Nation-Building, 1540–1840* (Tuscaloosa: University of Alabama Press, 2022). A sequence of anthologies published over the last quarter-century represented and influenced advancement in the

study of Native American women: Nancy Shoemaker, ed., *Negotiators of Change: Historical Perspectives on Native American Women* (New York: Routledge, 1995); Theda Perdue, ed., *Sifters: Native American Women's Lives* (New York: Oxford University Press, 2001); Kugel and Murphy, eds., *Native Women's History in Eastern North America before 1900;* Carol Williams, ed., *Indigenous Women and Work: From Labor to Activism* (Champaign: University of Illinois Press, 2012). Also see Ann M. Little, "Gender and Sexuality in the North American Borderlands, 1492–1848," *History Compass* 7, no. 6 (2009): 1606–15.

6. Angela Pulley Hudson with paintings by Hatty Ruth Miller, "Unsettling Histories of the South," *Southern Cultures* 25 (Fall 2019): 30–45.

7. Fred B. Kniffen, Hiram F. Gregory, and George A. Stokes, *The Historic Indian Tribes of Louisiana: From 1542 to the Present* (Baton Rouge: Louisiana State University Press, 1987), 150–51; Dayna Bowker Lee and H. F. Gregory, eds., *The Work of Tribal Hands: Southeastern Indian Split Cane Basketry* (Natchitoches, LA: Northwestern State University Press, 2006).

8. Tiya Miles, *All That She Carried: The Journey of Ashley's Sack, a Black Family Keepsake* (New York: Random House, 2021); Rayna Green, "Red Earth People and Southeastern Basketry," in *Basketmakers: Meaning and Form in Native American Baskets,* ed. Linda Mowatt, Howard Morphy, and Penny Dransart (Oxford: Pitt Rivers Museum Monograph 5, 1992), 11–17, quote from 16. For my formative thoughts about American Indian basketry and the study of material culture, see Daniel H. Usner, "An Ethnohistory of Things: Or, How to Treat California's Canastromania" [ASE Presidential Address 2011], *Ethnohistory* 59 (Summer 2012): 441–63.

9. Alyssa Mt. Pleasant, Caroline Wigginton, and Kelly Wisecup, "Materials and Methods in Native American and Indigenous Studies: Completing the Turn," *William and Mary Quarterly* 3d ser. 75 (April 2018): 207–36. Caroline Wigginton's *Indigenuity: Native Craftwork and the Art of American Literatures* (Chapel Hill: University of North Carolina Press, 2022) is a groundbreaking example of this methodology.

10. Thomas E. Emerson, *Cahokia and the Archaeology of Power* (Tuscaloosa: University of Alabama Press, 1997), 196–212; F. Kent Reilly III, "People of Earth, People of Sky: Visualizing the Sacred in Native American Art of the Mississippian Period," in *Hero, Hawk, and Open Hand: American Indian Art of the Ancient Midwest and South* (Chicago: Art Institute of Chicago, 2004), 124–37.

11. David D. Smits, "The 'Squaw Drudge': A Prime Index of Savagism," *Ethnohistory* 29 (Autumn 1982): 281–306.

12. Essays about women in various Native American nations edited and introduced by Carol Williams in *Indigenous Women and Work* are especially helpful for gaining comparative insight and interpretation.

13. Geary Hobson, Janet McAdams, and. Kathryn Walkiewicz, eds., *The People Who Stayed: Southeastern Indian Writing after Removal* (Norman: University of Oklahoma Press, 2010).

14. LeAnne Howe, *Shell Shaker* (San Francisco: Aunt Lute Books, 2001), 221. For insight into Howe's treatment of Choctaw people's ongoing relationship with the Deep South, see

Kirstin L. Squint, "Choctaw Homescapes: LeAnne Howe's Gulf Coast," *Mississippi Quarterly* 66 (Winter 2013): 115–38.

1. ENSLAVEMENT AND EXCHANGE IN THE COLONIAL SOUTH

1. Patricia Galloway, "Natchez Matrilineal Kinship: Du Pratz and the Woman's Touch," in *Practicing Ethnohistory: Mining Archives, Hearing Testimony, Constructing Narratives* (Lincoln: University of Nebraska Press, 2006); Gordon M. Sayre, "Natchez Ethnohistory Revisited: New Manuscript Sources from Le Page du Pratz and Dumont de Montigny," *Louisiana History* 50 (Fall 2009): 407–36.

2. For Le Page du Pratz's collection and shipment of plants for study in France, as requested by the Company of the Indies, see Antoine Le Page Du Pratz, *Histoire de la Louisiane,* 3 vols. (Paris: Du Bure, Delaguette, Lambert, 1758), I, 211–12. Native American contributions to the knowledge, circulation, and collection of Lower Mississippi Valley plants are discussed in Lake Douglas, *Public Spaces, Private Gardens: A History of Designed Landscapes in New Orleans* (Baton Rouge: Louisiana State University Press, 2011), 135–47; and Mary Louise Christovich and Roulhac Bunkley Toledano, *Garden Legacy* (New Orleans: Historic New Orleans Collection, 2016), 50–53, 61–67.

3. Allan Gallay, *The Indian Slave Trade: The Rise of the English Empire in the American South, 1670–1717* (New Haven, CT: Yale University Press, 2002); Gallay, ed., *Indian Slavery in Colonial America* (Lincoln: University of Nebraska Press, 2009). The state of knowledge about Indian slavery toward the end of the twentieth century was represented in Yashuhide Kawashima, "Indian Servitude in the Northeast," Peter H. Wood, "Indian Servitude in the Southeast," Albert H. Schroeder and Omer C. Stewart, "Indian Servitude in the Southwest," and Robert F. Heizer, "Indian Servitude in California," *Smithsonian Handbook of North American Indians, Volume 4: History of Indian-White Relations,* ed. Wilcomb E. Washburn (Washington DC: U.S. Government Printing Office, 1988), 404–16.

4. Louis Pelzer, Review of Almon Wheeler Lauber's *Indian Slavery in Colonial Times within the Present Limits of the United States,* in *Mississippi Valley Historical Review* 1 (June 1914): 123–24. Likewise, it is no longer possible to accept words written by Vine Deloria Jr. in *Custer Died for Your Sins:* "It is fortunate that we [Native Americans] were never slaves. We gave up land instead of life and labor." For a remarkable Western Hemispheric synthesis of the latest scholarship see Andrés Reséndez, *The Other Slavery: The Uncovered Story of Indian Enslavement in America* (Boston: Houghton Mifflin Harcourt, 2016), where he writes on page 5: "If we were to add up all the Indian slaves taken in the New World from the time of Columbus to the end of the nineteenth century, the figure would run somewhere between 2.5 and 5 million slaves."

5. Juliana Barr, *Peace Came in the Form of a Woman: Indians and Spaniards in the Texas Borderlands* (Chapel Hill: University of North Carolina Press, 2007); Christina Snyder, *Slavery in Indian Country: The Changing Face of Captivity in Early America* (Cambridge, MA: Harvard University Press, 2010).

6. Gregory A. Waselkov, Peter H. Wood, and Thomas Hatley, eds., *Powhatan's Mantle: Indians in the Colonial Southeast* (Lincoln: University of Nebraska Press, 1989, revised and expanded in 2006). For assessment of the historiography since the 1980s, see Alejandra Dubcovsky and Daniel H. Usner, "Native Homelands, Imperial Rivalries, and Contested Legacies of the Early South," in *Reinterpreting Southern Histories: Essays in Historiography*, ed. Craig Thompson Friend and Lorri Glover (Baton Rouge: Louisiana State University Press, 2020), 15–42.

7. James Axtell, *The Indians' New South: Cultural Change in the Colonial Southeast* (Baton Rouge: Louisiana State University Press, 1997), 4, 24. A sample of scholarship spatially expanding the range of early American history can be found in Juliana Barr and Edward Countryman, eds., *Contested Spaces of Early America* (Philadelphia: University of Pennsylvania Press, 2014); and Cécile Vidal, ed., *Louisiana: Crossroads of the Atlantic World* (Philadelphia: University of Pennsylvania Press, 2014).

8. These chronological and geographical leanings in the literature are made evident in April Lee Hatfield, "Colonial Southeastern Indian History," *Journal of Southern History* 73 (August 2007): 567–78.

9. James H. Merrell, *The Indians' New World: Catawbas and Their Neighbors from European Contact through the Era of Removal* (Chapel Hill: University of North Carolina Press, 1989); Alyssa Mt. Pleasant, Caroline Wigginton, and Kelly Wisecup, "Materials and Methods in Native American and Indigenous Studies: Completing the Turn," *William and Mary Quarterly* 3d ser. 75 (April 2018): 207–36. For examples of recently published innovative work on these communities, see Kristalyn Marie Shefveland, *Anglo-Native Virginia: Trade, Conversion, and Indian Slavery in the Old Dominion, 1646–1722* (Athens: University of Georgia Press, 2016); Mary Elizabeth Fitts, *Fit for War: Sustenance and Order in the Mid-Eighteenth-Century Catawba Nation* (Gainesville: University Press of Florida, 2017); Denise I. Bossy, ed., *The Yamasee Indians: From Florida to South Carolina* (Lincoln: University of Nebraska Press, 2018); and Elizabeth Ellis, *The Great Power of Small Nations: Indigenous Diplomacy in the Gulf South* (Philadelphia: University of Pennsylvania Press, 2022).

10. Theda Perdue, *"Mixed Blood" Indians: Racial Construction in the Early South* (Athens: University of Georgia Press, 2003); Micheline E. Pesantubbee, *Choctaw Women in a Chaotic World: The Clash of Cultures in the Colonial Southeast* (Albuquerque: University of New Mexico Press, 2005); Andrew K. Frank, *Creeks and Southerners: Biculturalism on the Early American Frontier* (Lincoln: University of Nebraska Press, 2005); Joshua Piker, *Okfuskee: A Creek Indian Town in Colonial America* (Cambridge, MA: Harvard University Press, 2004); Michelle LeMaster, *Brothers Born of One Mother: British-Native American Relations in the Colonial Southeast* (Charlottesville: University of Virginia Press, 2012); Shefveland, *Anglo-Native Virginia;* Céline Carayon, *Eloquence Embodied: Nonverbal Communication among French and Indigenous Peoples in the Americas* (Chapel Hill: University of North Carolina Press, 2019); Ellis, *Great Power of Small Nations.*

11. Robin A. Beck, Gayle J. Fritz, Heather A. Lapham, David G. Moore, and Christopher B. Rodning, "The Politics of Provisioning: Food and Gender at Fort San Juan de

Joara, 1566–1568," *American Antiquity* 81 (January 2016): 3–26. For a study of the Catawbas that uses archaeological analysis of material objects to track their formation during the eighteenth century and the role of women in the process, see Fitts, *Fit for War.*

12. Karen Ordahl Kupperman, *Pocahontas and the English Boys: Caught between Cultures in Early Virginia* (New York: New York University Press, 2019), quote from page 24.

13. Richebourg Gaillard McWilliams, trans. and ed., *Fleur de Lys and Calumet: Being the Pénicaut Narrative of French Adventure in Louisiana* (Baton Rouge: Louisiana State University Press, 1953), 70–72, 101–02, 216–20; Bienville to Pontchartrain, February 25, 1708, *Mississippi Provincial Archives: French Dominion,* ed. Dunbar Rowland, Godfrey Sanders, and Patricia K. Galloway (vols. 1–3, Jackson: Mississippi Department of Archives and History, 1929–32; vols. 4–5, Baton Rouge: Louisiana State University Press, 1984), III, 38.

14. Daniel H. Usner, "Chitimacha Diplomacy and Commerce in Colonial Louisiana," *Louisiana History* 62 (Spring 2021): 133–76, especially 136–41.

15. *Pénicaut Narrative,* 159. For scholarship on the "shatter zone" in the Lower Mississippi Valley, see Robbie Ethridge, *From Chicaza to Chickasaw: The European Invasion and the Transformation of the Mississippian World, 1540–1715* (Chapel Hill: University of North Carolina Press, 2010); and Ethridge and Sheri M. Shuck-Hall, eds., *Mapping the Mississippian Shatter Zone: The Colonial Indian Slave Trade and Regional Instability in the American South* (Lincoln: University of Nebraska Press, 2009).

16. Gregory A. Waselkov and Bonnie L. Gums, eds., *Plantation Archaeology at Rivière aux Chiens, ca. 1725–1848* (Mobile: University of South Alabama Center for Archaeological Studies, 2000), 35; H. Sophie Burton and F. Todd Smith, *Colonial Natchitoches: A Creole Community on the Louisiana-Texas Frontier* (College Station: Texas A&M University Press, 2008), 30, 39–41, 55; Dayna Bowker Lee, "From Captives to Kin: Indian Slavery and Changing Social Identities on the Louisiana Colonial Frontier," in *Native American Adoption, Captivity, and Slavery in Changing Contexts,* ed. Max Carocci and Stephanie Pratt (New York, 2012), 79–96. For consideration of evidence indicating that Natchez people enslaved and shipped to Saint-Domingue had descendants who maintained a Natchez identity within that island's society, see Noel E. Smyth, "The Obfuscation of Native American Presence in the French Atlantic: Natchez Indians in Saint Domingue, 1731–1791," *Ethnohistory* 69 (July 2022): 265–85.

17. Ellis, *Great Power of Small Nations.*

18. In "Columbus Meets Pocahontas in the American South," *Southern Cultures* 3 (Spring 1997): 4–21, Theda Perdue provides insightful guidance into how European men misrepresented and exploited the sexuality of Indigenous women and also shed light on the reality of Native sexual and marriage rules.

19. George Edward Milne, *Natchez Country: Indians, Colonists, and the Landscapes of Race in French Louisiana* (Athens: University of Georgia Press, 2015), 45–51, 164, 202; Linda Carol Jones, *The Shattered Cross: French Catholic Missionaries on the Mississippi River, 1698–1725* (Baton Rouge: Louisiana State University Press, 2020), 169–79.

20. Bienville to Pontchartrain, August 10, 1733, *Mississippi Provincial Archives: French Dominion,* III, 624–25.

21. Régis du Roullet to Périer, February 21, 1731, Louboey to Maurepas, February 8, 1746, *Mississippi Provincial Archives: French Dominion,* IV, 61–62, 259–60.

22. Jeffrey Ostler, *Surviving Genocide: Native Nations and the United States from the American Revolution to Bleeding Kansas* (New Haven, CT: Yale University Press, 2019), 12–17.

23. Jean-Jacques-Blaise d'Abbadie's journal entry for September 6, 1763, in *A Comparative View of French Louisiana, 1690 and 1762: The Journals of Pierre Le Moyne d'Iberville and Jean-Jacques-Blaise d'Abbadie,* trans. and ed. Carl A. Brasseaux (Lafayette: University of Southwestern Louisiana Press, 1979), 100–102.

24. Edward Mease, "Narrative of a Journey through West Florida," in "Peter Chester, Third Governor of the Province of West Florida under British Dominion, 1770–1781," ed. Eron O. Rowland, *Publications of the Mississippi Historical Society,* Centenary Series, 5 (1925): 68–70.

25. Le Page du Pratz, *Histoire de la Louisiane,* II, 86–87. The ubiquity of Indigenous uses of bear oil and the extent of its consumption by colonial consumers have recently been featured in Heather A. Lapham and Gregory A. Waselkov, eds., *Bears: Archaeological and Ethnohistorical Perspectives in Native Eastern North America* (Gainesville: University of Florida Press, 2020). For the southeast, see especially Waselkov, "Ethnohistorical and Ethnographic Sources on Bear-Human Relationships in Native Eastern North America," pp. 16–47; and Heidi M. Altman, Tanya M. Peres, and J. Matthew Compton, "Better than Butter: *Yona Go'i,* Bear Grease in Cherokee Culture," pp. 193–216.

26. Josef Pauli to Esteban Miró, 1790 [no month and day], in *Spain in the Mississippi Valley, 1765–1794,* trans. and ed. Lawrence Kinnaird, 3 vols. (Washington, DC: U.S. Government Printing Office, 1946–1949), II, 382–83; Charles César Robin, *Voyage to Louisiana, 1803–1805,* trans. Stuart O. Landry Jr. (New Orleans: Pelican Publishing Co., 1966), 151.

27. See Smits, "The 'Squaw' Drudge," for analysis of this weaponization of women's work. Thankfully, historians are now studying in detail the actual role played by Indigenous women's agriculture in their own societies and in colonial relations. The influence on historical events of Native women's role as producers of wild and domestic plants is skillfully demonstrated in Susan Sleeper-Smith, *Indigenous Prosperity and American Conquest: Indian Women of the Ohio River Valley, 1690–1792* (Chapel Hill: University of North Carolina Press, 2018).

28. Robin, *Voyage to Louisiana,* 128.

29. Richebourg Gaillard McWilliams, trans. and ed., *Iberville's Gulf Journals* (University: University of Alabama Press, 1981), 56.

30. Robin, *Voyage to Louisiana,* 128; Kevin Joel Berland, ed. *The Dividing Line Histories of William Byrd II* (Chapel Hill: University of North Carolina Press, 2013), 144.

31. Mart A. Stewart, "From King Cane to King Cotton: Razing Cane in the Old South," *Environmental History* 12 (January 2007): 59–79; Georgann Eubanks, *Saving the Wild South: The Fight for Native Plants on the Brink of Extinction* (Chapel Hill: University of North Carolina Press, 2021), 156–76.

32. Jean-François-Benjamin Dumont de Montigny, *The Memoir of Lieutenant Dumont, 1715–1747: A Sojourner in the French Atlantic,* trans. Gordon M. Sayre, ed. Sayre and Carla Zecher (Chapel Hill: University of North Carolina Press, 2012), 220–21.

33. This description of Chitimacha basketry is drawn from John R. Swanton, *Indian Tribes of the Lower Mississippi Valley and Adjacent Coast of the Gulf of Mexico* (Washington, DC: Government Printing Office, 1911), 347–48; Caroline Dormon, "The Last of the Cane Basket Makers," *Holland's, The Magazine of the South* (October 1931): 13, 66; Hiram F. Gregory and Clarence H. Webb, "Chitimacha Basketry," *Louisiana Archeology* 2 (1975): 28–33; John Paul Darden, Scarlett Darden, and Melissa Darden Brown, "In the Family Tradition: A Conversation with Three Chitimacha Basketmakers," in *The Work of Tribal Hands: Southeastern Indian Split Cane Basketry,* ed. Dayna Bowker Lee and H. F. Gregory (Natchitoches, LA: Northwestern State University Press), 29–41. What Holy Woman taught the Chitimachas about how to cut and weave the cane was told by Chief Benjamin Paul to linguist Morris Swadesh during the 1930s. "The Origin of Basket Weaving" (Story A13), Morris Swadesh, Field Notes on Chitimacha 1930–34, Committee on Native American Languages, American Philosophical Society, Philadelphia.

34. Brooks B. Ellwood, Sophie Warny, Rebecca A. Hackworth, Suzanne H. Ellwood, Jonathan H. Tompkins, Samuel J. Bentley, Dewitt H. Braud, and Geoffrey C. Clayton, "The LSU Campus Mounds, with Construction Beginning at -11,000 BP, Are the Oldest Known Extant Man-Made Structures in the Americas," *American Journal of Science* 322 (June 2022): 795–827.

35. Gerard Fowke, "Archaeological Investigations—II," *Forty-Fourth Annual Report of the Bureau of Ethnology to the Secretary of the Smithsonian Institution 1926–1927* (Washington, DC: U.S. Government Printing Office, 1928), 423–24.

36. George I. Quimby, *The Medora Site, West Baton Rouge Parish, Louisiana* (Chicago: Field Museum of Natural History, 1951), 99–100; Quimby, *The Bayou Goula Site, Iberville Parish, Louisiana* (Chicago: Field Museum of Natural History, 1957), 110, 147–56; Jeffrey S. Girard, *The Caddos and Their Ancestors: Archaeology and the Native People of Northwest Louisiana* (Baton Rouge: Louisiana State University Press, 2018), 50–52.

37. *Pénicaut Narrative,* 14–15; Stouff and Twitty, *Sacred Chitimacha Indian Beliefs,* 37, 53; Kniffen, Gregory, and Stokes, *Historic Indian Tribes of Louisiana,* 146.

38. "Letter from Father le Petit, Missionary, to Father d'Avaugour, Procurator of the Missions in North America," in *Jesuit Relations and Allied Documents: Travels and Explorations of the Jesuit Missionaries in New France, 1610–1791,* ed. Reuben Gold Thwaites (Cleveland: Burrows Brothers, 1900), vol. 68, pp. 121–22.

39. *Memoir of Lieutenant Dumont,* 220–21, 362, 382–83. Although Dumont never described Indian women actually weaving their baskets, he did write a detailed account of their manufacture of clay ceramics and marveled over "plates and bowls that are pretty and very well made." *Memoir,* 350–51. He even published a separate essay on the subject, "Poterie des peuples de la Louisiane, par M.D.M.," *Journal économique* (November 1752): 133–35.

40. "Complaint of Hottleboyau," Minutes of 23 January 1716/17, *The Colonial Records of South Carolina, Series 2: The Indian Books,* ed. William L. McDowell (Columbia: South Carolina Department of Archives and History, 1956), I, 149–50. For other examples of basketry in possession of British colonists, see Michelle LeMaster, *Brothers Born of One Mother: British-Native American Relations in the Colonial Southeast* (Charlottesville: University of Virginia Press, 2012), 130–33.

41. David. I. Bushnell Jr., "The Sloane Collection in the British Museum," *American Anthropologist* n.s. 8 (1906): 678–79. For a deeper look into the significance of this Cherokee basket, see Amanda Thompson, "A Sustaining Cherokee Basket: Colonial Inscription and Indigenous Resistance," *Sequitur* 6 (2020) [an online journal housed within Boston University's Department of History of Art and Architecture], https://www.bu.edu/sequitur/2020/10/18/a-sustaining-cherokee-basket-colonial-and-indigenous-resistance, accessed June 1, 2022.

42. Jessica Yirush Stern, *The Lives in Objects: Native Americans, British Colonists, and Cultures of Labor and Exchange in the Southeast* (Chapel Hill: University of North Carolina Press, 2017), 18–19, 124–25.

43. John Lawson, *A New Voyage to Carolina,* edited with an introduction and notes by Hugh Talmadge Lefler (Chapel Hill: University of North Carolina Press, 1967), 34–35, 75, 195–96.

44. *Dividing Line Histories of William Byrd II,* 121, 380; Mark Catesby, *The Natural History of Carolina, Florida, and the Bahama Islands* (London: Benjamin White, 1771), xi.

45. James Adair, *The History of the American Indians* (London: Edward and Charles Dilly, 1775), 424. Lieutenant Henry Timberlake saw enough Cherokee basketry into the 1760s to consider it among the "proofs of their ingenuity." Duane H. King, ed., *The Memoirs of Lieutenant Henry Timberlake: The Story of a Soldier, Adventurer, and Emissary to the Cherokees, 1756–1765* (Cherokee, NC: Museum of the Cherokee Indian Press, 2007), 32.

46. *Memoir of Lieutenant Dumont, 383.*

47. Peter H. Wood, "All in One Basket," *Avery Messenger* 6 (Fall 2008): 9–15; Investigation of a Theft Committed at Sr. Delaunay's, "Records of the Superior Council," *Louisiana Historical Quarterly* 12 (October 1929), 651–52. For archaeological evidence of Indian ceramics being used by colonists even for decoration and display as well as for cooking and storage, see Shannon Lee Dawdy and Christopher N. Matthews, "Colonial and Early Antebellum New Orleans," *Archaeology of Louisiana,* ed. Mark A. Rees (Baton Rouge: Louisiana State University Press, 2010), 273–305.

48. *Travels of William Bartram,* ed. Mark Van Doren (New York: Dover Publications, 1928), 271–72. For some context of Bartram's visit to the Lower Mississippi Valley in 1775, see Taylor McGaughy, "Bartram's Westerly Wanderings: Economic Transactions in *Travels,*" and Daniel H. Usner, "'A Prospect of the Grand Sublime': An Atlantic World Borderland Seen and Unseen by William Bartram," in *The Attention of a Traveller: Essays on William Bartram's Travels and Legacy* (Tuscaloosa: University of Alabama Press, 2022), 1–18, 19–37.

49. Donald G. Hunter, "The Choctaw and the Small Nations of Rapides, 1763–1860," *Southern Studies* 8 (Summer/Fall 1997): 41–92. For studies of the regional trade jargon, see James M. Crawford, *The Mobilian Trade Language* (Knoxville: University of Tennessee Press, 1978); and Emanuel J. Drechsel, *Mobilian Jargon: Linguistic and Sociohistorical Aspects of a Native American Pidgin* (Oxford: Clarendon Press, 1997).

50. For a thorough analysis of this population in the English colonies, where historians have for a long time underestimated its size and influence, see A. B. Wilkinson, *Blurring the Lines of Race and Freedom: Mulattoes and Mixed Bloods in English Colonial America* (Chapel Hill: University of North Carolina Press, 2020). For Louisiana, see Jennifer M. Spear, *Race, Sex, and Social Order in Early New Orleans* (Baltimore: Johns Hopkins University Press, 2009).

51. Stephen Webre, "The Problem of Indian Slavery in Spanish Louisiana, 1769–1803," *Louisiana History* 25 (Spring 1984): 117–35, quote from 129–30. Petitioning for freedom based on claims of Indian descent was not unique to Louisiana. In other parts of the Revolutionary era South, especially in Virginia, similar efforts were underway. See Ariela J. Gross and Alejandro de la Fuente, "Slaves, Free Blacks, and Race in the Legal Regimes of Cuba, Louisiana, and Virginia: A Comparison," *North Carolina Law Review* 91, no. 5 (2013): 1699–1756, especially pp. 1747–50. In an oft-cited case from the St. Louis area, it took three decades of litigation before the grandchildren of a Native American woman finally won their freedom. That Indian ancestor was a Natchez woman captured during the French war against her people and sold into slavery. In the 1740s she gave birth to Marie Jean Scypion, whose father was an enslaved man of African descent. Even after Louisiana came under Spanish rule and despite her repeated claims, Marie Jean Scypion and her three daughters were kept in slavery by prominent members of St. Louis society. After her death in 1802, Scypion's daughters pursued a series of stymied lawsuits until finally gaining freedom in the 1830s. William E. Foley, "Slave Freedom Suits before Dred Scott," *Missouri Historical Review* 79 (October 1984): 1–23.

52. Kathleen DuVal, *Independence Lost: Lives on the Edge of the American Revolution* (New York: Random House, 2015); Hunter, "Choctaw and the Small Nations of Rapides," 46, 54.

53. Gertrude C. Taylor, "Early History of the Chitimacha," *Attakapas Gazette* 16 (Summer 1981): 68; Donald Juneau, "The Light of Dead Stars," *American Indian Law Review* 11, no. 1 (1983): 1–55; Usner, "Chitimacha Diplomacy and Commerce in Colonial Louisiana," 160–62.

54. Ralph Ellison, *Going to the Territory* (New York: Random House, 1986), 125.

2. DISPOSSESSION AND SURVIVAL IN THE PLANTATION SOUTH

1. Claiborne to Jefferson, October 5, 1808, in *Letter Books of W. C. C. Claiborne, 1801–1816*, ed. Dunbar Rowland (Jackson, MS: State Department of Archives and History, 1917), IV, 223–24; Daniel Clark, An Account of the Indian Tribes in Louisiana, in *The Territorial*

Papers of the United States. Volume IX: The Territory of Orleans, 1803–1812, comp. and ed. Clarence Edwin Carter (Washington, DC: Government Printing Office, 1940), 62–63.

2. Act erecting Louisiana into two territories, and providing for the temporary government thereof, March 26, 1804, in *Territorial Papers of the United States. Volume IX*, 212–13.

3. Donald G. Hunter, "The Choctaw and the Small Nations of Rapides, 1763–1860," *Southern Studies* 8 (Summer/Fall 1997): 58–69; Julia Lewandoski, "Property, Migration, and Survival: Petites Nations and Land in Late Spanish and Early U.S. Louisiana," paper presented at the Allen Morris Forum on the Native South, December 14, 2021.

4. Dayna Bowker Lee, "The Historic Houma of Louisiana: 1699–1835," *Southern Studies* 8 (Summer/Fall 1997): 119–55; J. Daniel D'Oney, *A Kingdom of Water: Adaptation and Survival in the Houma Nation* (Lincoln: University of Nebraska Press, 2020), 55–77; Hiram F. Gregory, "Jena Band of Louisiana Choctaw," *American Indian Journal* 3 (February 1977): 2–16; Donald G. Hunter, "The Choctaw and the Small Nations of Rapides, 1763–1860," *Southern Studies* 8 (Summer/Fall 1997): 41–92; Brian Klopotek, "The Tunicas and Biloxis Navigate the American Era," in *The Tunica-Biloxi Tribe: Its Culture and People,* ed. Brian Klopotek, John D. Barbry, Donna M. Pierite, and Elizabeth Pierite-Mora (2nd edition, Tunica-Biloxi Tribe of Louisiana, 2017), 21–29.

5. Claudio Saunt, *Unworthy Republic: The Dispossession of Native Americans and the Road to Indian Territory* (New York: W. W. Norton & Co., 2020); Samantha Seeley, *Race, Removal, and the Right to Remain: Migration and the Making of the United States* (Chapel Hill: University of North Carolina Press, 2021). For a thorough and thoughtful assessment of the recent scholarship on removal, see Christina Snyder, "Many Removals: Re-evaluating the Arc of Indigenous Dispossession," *Journal of the Early Republic* 41 (Winter 2021): 623–50.

6. In *Settler Memory: The Disavowal of Indigeneity and the Politics of Race in the United States* (Chapel Hill: University of North Carolina Press, 2021), xiii, Kevin Bruyneel examines how "a settler society habitually reproduces memories of Indigenous people's history and of settler colonial violence and dispossession and in the same moment undercuts the political relevance of this memory by disavowing the presence of Indigenous people as contemporary agents and of settler colonialism as a persistent shaping force." For an exemplary approach to forms of both White disavowal and Native presence that occurred in another region during the nineteenth century, see Jean M. O'Brien, *Firsting and Lasting: Writing Indians Out of Existence in New England* (Minneapolis: University of Minnesota Press, 2010).

7. Jane Dinwoodie, "Evading Indian Removal in the American South," *Journal of American History* (June 2021): 17–41, quote from 40–41. In order to recover their identity from the colonial sobriquet, tribal members would eventually replace "Creek Nation" with "Muscogee Nation" as their official name.

8. See Malcolm Ebright, Rick Hendricks, and Richard W. Hughes, *Four Square Leagues: Pueblo Indian Land in New Mexico* (Albuquerque: University of New Mexico Press, 2014); and Juliana Hu Pegues, *Space-Time Colonialism: Alaska's Indigenous and Asian Entanglements* (Chapel Hill: University of North Carolina Press, 2021).

9. For exemplary approaches to these means of enacting sovereignty, see Dawn G. Marsh, *A Lenape among the Quakers: The Life of Hannah Freeman* (Lincoln: University of Nebraska Press, 2014); Margaret Huettl, "Treaty Stories: Reclaiming the Unbroken History of Lac Courte Oreilles Ojibwe Sovereignty," *Ethnohistory* 68 (April 2021): 215–36.

10. Alice Littlefield, "Making a Living: Anishinaabe Women in Michigan's Changing Economy," in *Indigenous Women and Work: From Labor to Activism,* ed. Carol Williams (Urbana: University of Illinois Press, 2012), 46–59; Susan Roy and Ruth Taylor, "'We Were Real Skookum Women': The shishálh Economy and the Logging Industry on the Pacific Northwest Coast," in *Indigenous Women and* Work, 104–19; Beth H. Piatote, *Domestic Subjects: Gender, Citizenship, and Law in Native American Literature* (New Haven, CT: Yale University Press, 2013), 98, 102–3; Adriana Greci Green, "Anishinaabe Gathering Rights and Market Arts: The Contribution of the WPA Indian Handicraft Project in Michigan," in *Tribal Worlds: Critical Studies in American Indian Nation Building,* ed. Brian Hosmer and Larry Nesper (Albany: State University of New York Press, 2013), 219–51. In their essay, Roy and Taylor find the making of baskets from cedar trees among Pacific Northwest communities to have had a unifying effect similar to the centrality of rivercane basketry among southern Indians.

11. See Paige Raibmon, *Authentic Indians: Episodes of Encounter from the Late-Nineteenth-Century Northwest Coast* (Durham, NC: Duke University Press, 2005); Lisa Tanya Brooks, *The Common Pot: The Recovery of Native Space in the Northeast* (Minneapolis: University of Minnesota Press, 2008); William J. Bauer Jr., *We Were All Like Migrant Workers Here: Work, Community, and Memory on California's Round Valley Reservation, 1850–1941* (Chapel Hill: University of North Carolina Press, 2009); Chantal Norrgard, *Seasons of Change: Labor, Treaty Rights, and Ojibwe Nationhood* (Chapel Hill: University of North Carolina Press, 2014); Joshua L. Reid, *The Sea Is My Country: The Maritime World of the Makahs* (New Haven, CT: Yale University Press, 2015); Micah A. Pawling, "*Wəlastəkwey* (Maliseet) Homeland: Waterscapes and Continuity within the Lower St. John River Valley, 1784–1900," *Acadiens* 46 (Summer/Autumn 2017): 5–34; Douglas K. Miller, *Indians on the Move: Native American Mobility and Urbanization in the Twentieth Century* (Chapel Hill: University of North Carolina Press, 2019).

12. T. N. Campbell, "Choctaw Subsistence: Ethnographic Notes from the Lincecum Manuscript," *Florida Anthropologist* 12 (March 1959): 9–24, is a useful glimpse into the traditional cycle of hunting, fishing, food collecting, and farming. For thoughtful discussions of the continuum in southern Indians' relationship with mounds, see LeAnne Howe, "Embodied Tribalography—First Installment," in *Choctalking on Other Realities* (San Francisco: Aunt Lute Books, 2013), 173–95, and "The Story of Movement: Natives and Performance Culture," in *The Oxford Handbook of Indigenous American* Literature, ed. James H. Cox and Daniel Heath Justice (New York: Oxford University Press, 2014), 250–65; Christina Snyder, "The Once and Future Moundbuilders," *Southern Cultures* 26 (Summer 2020): 96–116.

13. Clara Sue Kidwell, *Choctaws and Missionaries in Mississippi, 1818–1918* (Norman: University of Oklahoma Press, 1995); Jacqueline Anderson Matte, *They Say the Wind Is*

Red: The Alabama Choctaw—Lost in Their Own Land (rev. ed., Montgomery, AL: New South Books, 2018).

14. Daniel H. Usner, "Chitimacha Diplomacy and Commerce in Colonial Louisiana," *Louisiana History* 62 (Spring 2021): 133–76, especially 169–74; D'Oney, *Kingdom of Water,* 55–77.

15. Christopher Arris Oakley, *Keeping the Circle: American Indian Identity in Eastern North Carolina, 1885–2004* (Lincoln: University of Nebraska Press, 2005); Malinda Maynor Lowery, *The Lumbee Indians: An American Struggle* (Chapel Hill: University of North Carolina Press, 2018); Lance Greene, *Their Determination to Remain: A Cherokee Community's Resistance to the Trail of Tears in North Carolina* (Tuscaloosa: University of Alabama Press, 2022). Seminoles in the Everglades of south Florida formed comparable relationships with white merchants in surrounding towns. See Harry A. Kersey Jr., *Pelts, Plumes, and Hides: White Traders among the Seminole Indians, 1870–1930* (Gainesville: University Presses of Florida, 1975).

16. February 27, 1842, excerpt from the diary of Drury Paine Armstrong, quoted in Betty J. Duggan and Brett H. Riggs, *Studies in Cherokee Basketry* (Knoxville: Frank H. McClung Museum, University of Tennessee, 1991), 29.

17. John A. Watkins, "Choctaw Indians," John A. Watkins Manuscripts, Louisiana Research Collection, Howard-Tilton Memorial Library, Tulane University, New Orleans.

18. Entries for December 23, 1827, January 25, November 22, December 13, 1828, October 5, 1832, John Nevitt Diary, 1826–1832, Southern Historical Collection, Manuscripts Department, Affairs Library of the University of North Carolina at Chapel Hill.

19. Testimony of Ta nam pish ubbee, June 23, 1843, Case 262, Journal of Commissioner Graves, 1842–1843, Entry 275, Miscellaneous Choctaw Removal Records, ca. 1825–1858, National Archives.

20. Frederick Law Olmsted, *The Cotton Kingdom: A Traveller's Observations on Cotton and Slavery in the American Slave States* (1861), ed. Arthur M. Schlesinger (New York: Alfred A. Knopf, 1953), 367.

21. Susan Dabney Smedes, *Memorials of a Southern Planter* (Baltimore: Cushings & Bailey, 1887), 90–91. For other accounts of cotton picking by Choctaw women, see Fortescue Cuming, *Sketches of a Tour to the Western Country* (1810), ed. Reuben Gold Thwaites in *Early Western Travels, 1748–1846, Volume IV* (Cleveland: Arthur H. Clark Co., 1904), 351–52; Eliza Nutt to Rush Nutt, December 6, 1817, Rush Nutt Papers, Huntington Library, Art Collection, and Botanical Gardens, San Marino, California; Henry Bradshaw Fearon, *Sketches of America: A Narrative of a Journey of Five Thousand Miles through the Eastern and Western States of America* (London: Longman, Hurst, Rees, Morme, and Brown, 1819), 269.

22. Committee on Indian Affairs, House of Representatives, Report on Petitions from Citizens of Louisiana to Remove Indians, April 24, 1850, Reports of Committees, H.R. Report No. 276, 31st Congress, 1st Session, United States Congressional Serial Set, Serial No. 584.

23. Howard Corning, ed., *Journal of John James Audubon Made during His Trip to New Orleans in 1820–1821* (Boston: Club of Odd Volumes, 1929), 170; John Francis McDermott, ed., *Tixier's Travels on the Osage Prairies* (Norman: University of Oklahoma Press, 1940), 55–59, 81–82.

24. J. Hanno Deiler, The *Settlement of the German Coast* of Louisiana and the Creoles of German Descent (Philadelphia: American Germanica Press, 1909), 62; Meloncy C. Soniat, "The Tchoupitoulas Plantation," *Louisiana Historical Quarterly* 7 (April 1924): 309–10.

25. Clara Compton Raymond, "The Old Plantation Home" memoir in typescript, ca. 1930, p. 8, Louisiana Research Collection, Howard-Tilton Memorial Library, Tulane University. Raymond also pointed out that her brother was always overjoyed whenever his grandmother bought him a blowgun, "a long bamboo pole with arrows tipped with thistle down." She, on the other, could only admire it because it was "not lady-like" for girls to have boys' "play things."

26. François Dominique Rouquette, "The Choctaws," trans. Olivia Blanchard from original transcript, 11–12, François Dominique Rouquette Papers, Louisiana Research Collection, Howard-Tilton Memorial Library, Tulane University, New Orleans.

27. Dagmar Renshaw Lebreton, *Chahta-Ima: The Life of Adrien Emmanuel Rouquette* (Baton Rouge: Louisiana State University Press, 1947); Dominic Braud, "Père Rouquette, Missionnaire Extraordinaire: Father Adrien Rouquette's Mission to the Choctaw," in *Cross, Crozier, and Crucible: A Volume Celebrating the Bicentennial of a Catholic Diocese in Louisiana*, ed. Glenn R. Conrad (New Orleans: Archdiocese of New Orleans in cooperation with the Center for Louisiana Studies, 1993), 314–27; Rien Fertel, "Catholic Priest and Poet Adrien Rouquette Bridges the Atlantic Ocean," chapter 2 in his *Imagining the Creole City: The Rise of Literary Culture in Nineteenth-Century New Orleans* (Baton Rouge: Louisiana State University Press, 2014), 31–48.

28. Dayna Bowker Lee, with contributions by Audra L. Lee, Choctaw Communities along the Gulf Coast: Louisiana, Mississippi, and Alabama: Ethnographic Overview and Assessment of Mississippi Choctaw Communities along the Gulf Coast, Final report prepared for National Park Service and Federal Emergency Management Agency (New Orleans: Earth Search, Inc., 2009), 70.

29. Letters written by Adrien Rouquette and published in the *New Orleans Catholic Standard,* December 16, 1858, March 20, 1859, John Minor Wisdom Collection, 1710–1960, Louisiana Research Collection, Tulane University.

30. "Choctaws in Louisiana—A Talk with Father Rouquette about His Favorite Charge," *New Orleans Daily Picayune,* August 4, 1882.

31. "Choctaws in Louisiana—A Talk with Father Rouquette about His Favorite Charge," *New Orleans Daily Picayune,* August 4, 1882; Adrien Rouquette to John Dimitry, December 1, 1884, Adrien Rouquette Papers, 1842–1942, Louisiana Research Collection, Tulane University; "Personal and General Notes," *New Orleans Daily Picayune,* August 18, 1895; "Florida Parishes Fair," *New Orleans Daily Picayune,* November 29, 1897.

32. Blaise C. D'Antoni, "Chahta-Ima and St. Tammany's Choctaws," St. Tammany Historical Society, Inc., Mandeville, LA, 1986, typescript, Adrien Emmanuel Rouquette Papers, 1842–1942.

33. "Choctaws in Louisiana—A Talk with Father Rouquette about His Favorite Charge," *New Orleans Daily Picayune,* August 4, 1882.

34. "Catharine Cole's Letter," *New Orleans Daily Picayune,* March 1, 1883; "Father Rouquette: The Burial of the Poet Priest," *New Orleans Daily Picayune,* July 17, 1887.

35. Berhard, Duke of Saxe-Weimer Eisenach, *Travels through North America, during the Years 1825 and 1826,* 2 vols. (Philadelphia: Carey, Lea & Carey, 1828), II, 40, 50, 73; Fredrika Bremer, *The Homes of the New World: Impressions of America,* trans. Mary Howitt, 3 vols. (London: Arthur Hall, Virtue & Co., 1853), III, 19–21.

36. Matte, *They Say the Wind Is Red,* 57–64, 181–83.

37. Paul Alliot, "Historical and Political Reflections on Louisiana, July 1, 1803-April 13, 1804," in *Louisiana under the Rule of Spain, France, and the United States, 1785–1807,* ed. James A. Robertson, 2 vols. (Cleveland: Arthur Clark, 1911), 2:81–83.

38. Christian Schultz Jr., *Travels on an Inland Voyage through the States of New-York, Pennsylvania, Virginia, Ohio, Kentucky and Tennessee, and through the Territories of Indiana, Louisiana, Mississippi, and New-Orleans: Performed in the Years 1807 and 1808* (New York: Isaac Riley, 1810), II, 140–43; Cuming, *Sketches of a Tour,* 285–86.

39. James Morris Morgan, *Recollections of a Rebel Reefer* (Boston and New York: Houghton Mifflin, 1917), 3.

40. Marguerite C. Steckler, "The History of the Attacapa Indians for Elementary School Use" (M.A. thesis, George Peabody College for Teachers, 1932), 74; *Louisiana Democrat* (Alexandria, LA), February 21, 1884.

41. Mart A. Stewart, "From King Cane to King Cotton: Razing Cane in the Old South," *Environmental History* 12 (January 2007): 59–79, quote from 61.

42. Maria R. Audubon, *Audubon and His Journals,* with Zoölogical and Other Notes by Elliott Coues [2 volumes, originally published in 1897] (vol. 2, Freeport, NY: Books for Libraries Press, 1972), 267–73. Stopping at a camp of Osage and Shawnee Indians at the confluence of the Ohio and Mississippi rivers in 1810, Audubon depicted this scene: "We were now indeed in winter quarters, and we made the best of it. The Indians made baskets of cane, Mr. Pope played on the violin, I accompanied with the flute, the men danced to the tunes, and the squaws looked on and laughed, and the hunters smoked their pipes with such serenity as only Indians can, and I never regretted one day spent there." John James Audubon, *The Life of John James Audubon, the Naturalist,* Edited by His Widow. With an Introduction by James Grant Wilson (New York: G. P. Putnam & Sons, 1869), 43.

43. Smedes, *Memorials of a Southern Planter,* 90; Corinne L. Saucier, *The History of Avoyelles Parish, Louisiana* (New Orleans: Pelican Publishing Co., 1943), 14.

44. Bremer, *Homes of the New World,* III, 19–21.

45. Léon H. Grandjean, *Crayon Reproductions of Frémaux's New Orleans Characters* (New Orleans: Peychaud & Garcia, 1876), n.p.: text accompanying sketch "Choctaw Indian

Squaws" by engineer Léon J. Frémaux. Material evidence for nineteenth-century consumption of Louisiana Indian baskets can be found inside houses still standing, especially plantation houses that have survived—and even been restored—since then. Auctions of furnishings and decorative items belonging to estates handed down often include old Chitimacha and Choctaw baskets. Photographs of traditional homes in New Orleans and across south Louisiana that are periodically featured in publications also show Indian baskets sitting on mantles, tables, and floors—punctuating rooms furnished and decorated with period antiques and family heirlooms. Basketry still seen in houses as well as museums, therefore, represent intercultural transactions dating to the nineteenth century. See, for example, *Creole Houses: Traditional Homes of Old Louisiana,* Photographs by Steve Gross and Sue Daley, Commentary by John H. Lawrence, and Foreword by James Conaway (New York: Abrams, 2007), 69, 71, 85, 111, 114, 129, 130, 132, and 135.

46. Martha Reinhard Smallwood Field [Catharine Cole, pseud.], *The Story of the Old French Market* (New Orleans: New Orleans Coffee Company, ca. 1916), no pagination.

47. Charles Latrobe, *The Rambler in North America,* 2 vols. (London: R. B. Seeley and W. Burnside, 1836), II, 334.

48. William Gilmore Simms, "Oakatibbe, or the Choctaw Sampson" (initially published in 1841), in *Wigwam and the Cabin* (New York: Wiley & Putnam, 1845).

49. Alexis de Tocqueville, *Democracy in America, 2 vols.* [1835], trans. Henry Reeve (London: Longman, Green, Longman, and Roberts, 1862), vol. 1, 398–99.

50. James Smith, Esq., "The Maiden of Chitimachas" [Original Poetry], *Planters' Banner* (Franklin, LA), April 5, 1851. James Tinker Smith was born in St. Mary's Parish in 1816, orphaned in early boyhood, and sent by guardians to Scotland. After graduating from the University of Edinburgh, he returned to Louisiana and managed his family's plantations. Henry M. Gill, comp. and ed., *The South in Prose and Poetry* (New Orleans: F. F. Hansell & Bro., 1916), 42. Standard elements of white America's imaginary Indians appeared in Smith's "The Maiden of Chitimachas," which was published a few years ahead of Henry Wadsworth Longfellow's more famous verse, "The Song of Hiawatha." Before then, also worth noting, Longfellow had set another one of his epic poems along Bayou Teche—"Evangeline, A Tale of Acadia"—romanticizing the history and culture of the Chitimachas' Acadian neighbors.

51. Rebecca Solnit, *Savage Dreams: A Journey into the Hidden Wars of the American West,* 20th Anniversary Edition (Berkeley: University of California Press, 2014), 276–78.

52. Stefan Schöberlein, ed., *Walt Whitman's New Orleans: Sidewalk Sketches and Newspaper Rambles* (Baton Rouge: Louisiana State University Press, 2022), 13, 107; Lafcadio Hearn to Elizabeth H. E. Krehbiel, New Orleans, 1877, *The Life and Letters of Lafcadio Hearn,* ed. Elizabeth Bisland, 2 vols. (Boston: Houghton, Mifflin & Company, 1906), I, 168–69.

53. Laurel Thatcher Ulrich, *The Age of Homespun: Objects and Stories in the Creation of the American Myth* (New York: Alfred A. Knopf, 2001), 354–63, quote on 362. For my exploration into an array of vulnerable spaces in which American Indians worked and traded,

see Usner, *Indian Work: Language and Livelihood in Native American History* (Cambridge, MA: Harvard University Press, 2009).

54. Walter Prichard, Fred B. Kniffen, and Clair A. Brown, eds., "Southern Louisiana and Southern Alabama in 1819: The Journal of James Leander Cathcart," *Louisiana Historical Quarterly* 28 (July 1945): 850–51.

55. *Letters from John Pintard to His Daughter Eliza Noel Davidson 1816–1833,* 4 vols. (New York: New York Historical Society, 1940), II, 18. John Pintard himself had spent several months of 1801 in New Orleans.

56. Lady Emmeline Stuart-Wortley, *Travels in the United States, Etc. during 1849 and 1850* (New York: Harper & Brothers, 1851), 130–31. For more of my thoughts about how representation of Indigenous people was deployed in a wide range of shifting discourses in American culture, see Daniel H. Usner, *Indian Work: Language and Livelihood in Native American History* (Cambridge, MA: Harvard University Press, 2009).

57. Jennifer L. Morgan, "'Some Could Suckle over Their Shoulder': Male Travelers, Female Bodies, and the Gendering of Racial Ideology, 1500–1770," *William and Mary Quarterly* 3d ser. 54 (January 1997): 167–92.

58. *Tixier's Travels,* 55–59.

59. Victoria Welby-Gregory, *A Young Traveller's Journal of a Tour in North and South America during the Year 1850* (London: T. Bosworth, 1852), 137–39.

60. Alexander Beaufort Meek's "The Fawn of Pascagoula: or, the 'Chumpa' Girl of Mobile." A. B. Meek, *Romantic Passages in Southwestern History; including Orations, Sketches, and Essays, 2nd ed.* (New York: S. H. Goetzel & Co., 1857), 323–30.

61. Josiah Nott and George Glidden, *Types of Mankind* (Philadelphia, 1854); Reginal Horsman, *Josiah Nott of Mobile: Southerner, Physician, and Racial Theorist* (Baton Rouge: Louisiana State University Press, 1987), 58, 177.

62. Tiya Miles, *Ties That Bind: The Story of an Afro-Cherokee Family in Slavery and Freedom* (Berkeley: University of California Press, 2005), and *The House on Diamond Hill: A Cherokee Plantation Story* (Chapel Hill: University of North Carolina Press, 2010); Celia E. Naylor, *African Cherokees in Indian Territory: From Chattel to Citizens* (Chapel Hill: University of North Carolina Press, 2008); David A. Chang, *The Color of the Land: Race, Nation, and the Politics of Landownership in Oklahoma, 1832–1929* (Chapel Hill: University of North Carolina Press, 2010); Barbara Krauthamer, *Black Slaves, Indian Masters: Slavery, Emancipation, and Citizenship in the Native American South* (Chapel Hill: University of North Carolina Press, 2013). For a recent work that innovatively redirects this line of inquiry, see Christina Dickerson-Cousin, *Black Indians and Freedmen: The African Methodist Episcopal Church and Indigenous Americans, 1816–1916* (Urbana: University of Illinois Press, 2021). Work on Seminole-Black relations tend to be more inclusive of multiple dimensions of interaction. See Kevin Mulroy, *The Seminole Freedmen: A History* (Norman: University of Oklahoma Press, 2007; and Larry Eugene Rivers, *Rebels and Runaways: Slave Resistance in Nineteenth-Century Florida* (Champaign: University of Illinois Press, 2012).

63. Jeff Foret, *Race Relations at the Margins: Slaves and Poor Whites in the Antebellum Southern Countryside* (Baton Rouge: Louisiana State University Press, 2006).

64. Jack D. Forbes, "The Manipulation of Race, Caste, and Identity: Classifying Afro-Americans, Native Americans, and Red-Black People," *Journal of Ethnic Studies* 17 (Winter 1990): 1–51.

65. Carl A. Brasseux, Keith P. Fontenot, and Claude F. Oubre, *Creoles of Color in the Bayou Country* (Jackson: University Press of Mississippi, 1994); Warren Eugene Milteer Jr., *Beyond Slavery's Shadow: Free People of Color in the South* (Chapel Hill: University of North Carolina Press, 2021); Arica L. Coleman, *That the Blood Stay Pure: African Americans, Native Americans, and the Predicament of Race and Identity in Virginia* (Bloomington: Indiana University Press, 2013), 85; Lowery, *Lumbee Indians,* 67; Warren Milteer, "From Indians to Colored People: The Problem of Racial Categories and the Persistence of the Chowans in North Carolina," *North Carolina Historical Review* 93 (January 2016): 28–57.

66. For a sample of this language over time, see "Journal of James Leander Cathcart," 780–82, 823, 836–37; Paul Wilhelm, Duke of Württemberg, *Travels in North America, 1822–1824,* trans. W. Robert Nitske, ed. Savoie Lottinville (Norman: University of Oklahoma Press, 1973), 116–20; A. S. Gatschet, "The Shetimasha Indians of St. Mary's Parish, Southern Louisiana," *Transaction of the Anthropological Society of Washington* 2 (1883): 149; F. D. Richardson, "The Teche Country Fifty Years Ago," *Southern Bivouac: A Monthly Literary and Historical Magazine* 1 (March 1886): 597; Alcée Fortier, *Louisiana Studies: Literature, Customs and Dialects, History and Education* (New Orleans: F. F. Hansel & Bro., 1894), 165–66; John R. Ficklin, "The Indians of Louisiana," chap. 2 in *Standard History of New Orleans, Louisiana,* ed. Henry Rightor (Chicago: Lewis Publishing Company, 1900), 56–57.

67. Angela Pulley Hudson, "Removals and Remainders: Apaches and Choctaws in the Jim Crow South," *Journal of the Civil War Era* 11 (March 2021): 80–102. For detailed study of Apache experiences at Mount Vernon as well as at other military prisons in the South, see H. Henrietta Stockel, *Shame and Endurance: The Untold Story of the Chiricahua Apache Prisoners of War* (Tucson: University of Arizona Press, 2004).

68. *Report on Indians Taxed and Indians Not Taxed in the United States (Except Alaska) at the Eleventh Census: 1890* (Washington, DC: Government Printing Office, 1894), 131–32. Across the Gulf South region featured in this book, the 1890 census counted as "Indians self-supporting" 759 people in Alabama, 2,036 in Mississippi, 627 in Louisiana, plus 223 Alabama-Coushattas in Texas for a total of 3,645. Across the entire United States, "Indians self-supporting" totaled 58,806 people.

69. Richardson, "The Teche Country Fifty Years Ago," 594 and 597.

70. Usner, *American Indians in Early New Orleans,* 104–7.

71. *Historical Sketch Book and Guide to New Orleans and Environs,* Edited and Compiled by Several Leading Writers of the New Orleans Press (New York: Will H. Coleman, 1885), 169–70.

72. *New Orleans Times-Democrat,* April 6, 1885.

3. PERIL AND RECOVERY IN THE JIM CROW SOUTH

1. Christine Paul to Mary Bradford, March 9, 1905, Mary Bradford Papers, McIlhenny Company and Avery Island, Inc., Archives, Avery Island, LA.

2. Daniel H. Usner, *Weaving Alliances with Other Women: Chitimacha Indian Work in the New South* (Athens: University of Georgia Press, 2015).

3. *State v. Fulgence Chiqui* (No. 12,288), Supreme Court of Louisiana, January 4, 1897, *The Southern Reporter, Volume 21, Containing All the Decisions of the Supreme Courts of Alabama, Louisiana, Florida, Mississippi, Perment Edition, January 13–June 2, 1897* (St. Paul, MN: West Publishing Col, 1897), 513–14; Donald Juneau, "The Judicial Extinguishment of the Tunica Indian Tribe," *Southern University Law Review* 7(Fall 1980), 43–99, especially 73–86.

4. The impact of this craze for Indian things on American Indian communities in the South has received much less attention than that on Indigenous peoples in other regions. For understanding the wider movement and marketplace, the best analysis is Elizabeth Hutchinson, *The Indian Craze: Primitivism, Modernism, and Transculturation in American Art, 1890–1915* (Durham, NC: Duke University Press, 2009).

5. Christine Paul to Mary Bradford, September 10, 1899, Bradford Papers.

6. Roger Emile Stouff, *Native Waters: A Few Moments in a Small Wooden Boat* (Jeanerette, LA: Shadowfire Books, 2012), 113–14. For the effects of overflow in the Atchafalaya Basin and the government's response, see Craig E. Colten, *State of Disaster: A Historical Geography of Louisiana's Land Loss Crisis* (Baton Rouge: Louisiana State University Press, 2021), 99–111. In some parts of the region, incidentally, enough canebrakes still remained for sport hunters like Theodore Roosevelt to kill a black bear, as he put it, "after the fashion of the old Southern planters." In October 1907, the president was hosted on a bear hunt in north Louisiana by John M. Parker (a New Orleans merchant) and John A. McIlhenny (a brother of the McIlhenny sisters, veteran of the Rough Riders, and now member of the U.S. Civil Service Commission). Roosevelt called the tall canes standing so tightly together along Tensas Bayou "the refuge for hunted things," impossible to see farther than fifteen or twenty paces ahead and to penetrate without a heavy bush knife. After several days of searching without success and thanks to plenty of help from local black and white hunters, Roosevelt did manage with two shots to kill a large but lean female. As he confessed, however, "the cane was so thick that my sight was on it and not on the bear itself." Toward the end of his hunting trip in the area, Roosevelt observed a large mound. In a fashion commonly dismissive of contemporary Indians' connection to ancestral grounds, he wrote, "it had been built in the unknown past by those unknown people whom we call moundbuilders." Theodore Roosevelt, "In the Louisiana Canebrakes," chap. 12 in *Outdoor Pastimes of an American Hunter,* new and enlarged edition (New York: Charles Scribner's Sons, 1908), 360–90.

7. Usner, *Weaving Alliances with Other Women,* xii–xiv.

8. For examples of other work that emphasizes the agency of Indian women in their production for the arts and crafts market, see Sarah H. Hill, *Weaving New Worlds: South-*

eastern Cherokee Women and Their Basketry (Chapel Hill: University of North Carolina Press, 1997); Teresa J. Wilkins, *Patterns of Exchange: Navajo Weavers and Traders* (Norman: University of Oklahoma Press, 2008); Colette A. Hyman, *Dakota Women's Work: Creativity, Culture, and Exile* (St. Paul: Minnesota Historical Society Press, 2012); Jenny Tone-Pah-Hote, *Crafting an Indigenous Nation: Kiowa Expressive Culture in the Progressive Era* (Chapel Hill: University of North Carolina Press, 2019); and Megan A. Smetzer, *Painful Beauty: Tlingit Women, Beadwork, and the Art of Resilience* (Seattle: University of Washington Press, 2021).

9. Ledger sheet, November 16, 1901–December 14, 1904, Christine Paul to Mary Bradford, Mary Bradford Papers.

10. Margaret M. Bruchac, *Savage Kin: Indigenous Informants and American Anthropologists* (Tucson: University of Arizona Press, 2018), quote on 18. There is very little work on interaction between anthropologists and local patrons and supporters of Indian communities, although the study of other interpersonal relationships in anthropology is well developed, e.g. anthropologists' relations with spouses, partners, students, informants, and consultants. The correspondence held in the McIlhenny Company Archives makes it possible to catch glimpses of negotiation and interaction rarely seen. In addition to Mary Bradford's mediation between anthropologists and Chitimachas—which of course represented her own desire for status and influence—there is evidence of how members of the community perceived the ethnographic fieldwork and how they communicated their concerns and interests.

11. Valerie Sherer Mathes, ed., *The Women's National Indian Association: A History* (Albuquerque: University of New Mexico Press, 2015).

12. Daniel H. Usner, "From Bayou Teche to Fifth Avenue: Crafting a New Market for Chitimacha Indian Baskets," *Journal of Southern History* 69 (May 2013): 339–74.

13. Otis Tufton Mason, *Woman's Share in Primitive Culture* (New York: Appleton & Company, 1900). For inquiries into Progressive Era thought about craftsmanship, industry, and primitive society, see Michael Kammen, *Mystic Chords of Memory: The Transformation of Tradition in American Culture* (New York: Alfred A. Knopf, 1991), 254–82; T. J. Jackson Lears, *No Place of Grace: Antimodernism and the Transformation of American Culture, 1880–1920* (Chicago: University of Chicago Press, 1994), 60–96; Maurice Hamington, *The Social Philosophy of Jane Addams* (Urbana: University of Illinois Press, 2009), 159–61; Daniel E. Bender, *American Abyss: Savagery and Civilization in the Age of Industry* (Ithaca, NY: Cornell University Press, 2009), 23–24, 116–19.

14. Neltje Blanchan, "What the Basket Means to the Indian," chap. 15 in Mary White, *How to Make Baskets* (New York: Doubleday, Page & Co., 1901), 181–82, 188, 194.

15. Pauline Paul to Christine Paul, [month illegible] 25, 1909, and September 27, 1910, Chitimacha Papers, McIlhenny Company and Avery Island, Inc., Archives, Avery Island, LA; Christine Paul to Mary Bradford, November 21, 1909, Mary Bradford Papers.

16. "Hampton Incidents," *Southern Workman* 31 (March 1902): 164–65, quote from 164; Hill, *Weaving New Worlds*, 216–21; Virginia Moore Carney, *Eastern Band Cherokee Women:*

Cultural Persistence in Their Letters and Speeches (Knoxville: University of Tennessee Press, 2005), 101–7. Largely because of Swayney's employment at Hampton, the school received a donation of seventy-two rivercane baskets that had been made by Chitimacha women for the St. Louis world's fair in 1904. Neltje Doubleday facilitated this gift by persuading a national advocacy group named the Sequoya League to purchase the baskets from their weavers and bestow them to Hampton "in the hope that it will prove a source of inspiration and interest to the Indian girl students"—giving the school what is today one of the largest and most exquisite collection of Chitimacha baskets. "A Collection of Rare Baskets," *Southern Workman* 34 (July 1905): 377.

17. For an overview of the boarding school system, see David Wallace Adams, *Education for Extinction: American Indians and the Boarding School Experience, 1875–1928* (Lawrence: University Press of Kansas, 1995). The shift underway in how the schools treated Indian crafts is examined in Linda M. Waggoner, *Fire Light: The Life of Angel De Cora, Winnebago Artist* (Norman: University of Oklahoma Press, 2008).

18. Pauline Paul to Moses Friedman, January 10, 1914, Mamie Vilcan to Commissioner of Indian Affairs, January 24, 1914, Records of the Bureau of Indian Affairs, Central Classified Files, 1907–39, National Archives.

19. Delphine Stouff to Mark R. Harrington, January 22, 1912, Box 436, Records of the Bureau of Indian Affairs, Central Classified Files, 1907–1939.

20. Usner, *Weaving Alliances with Other Women*, 43–51.

21. Hill, *Weaving New Worlds;* Jay Precht, "Coushatta Basketry and Identity Politics: The Role of Pine-Needle Baskets in the Federal Recognition of the Coushatta Tribe of Louisiana," *Ethnohistory* 62 (January 2015): 145–67; Denise E. Bates, *Basket Diplomacy: Leadership, Alliance-Building, and Resilience among the Coushatta Tribe of Louisiana, 1884–1984* (Lincoln: University of Nebraska Press, 2020); Linda P. Langley and Denise E. Bates, *Louisiana Coushatta Basket Makers: Traditional Knowledge, Resourcefulness, and Artistry as a Means of Survival* (Baton Rouge: Louisiana State University Press, 2021).

22. *Report on Indians Taxed and Indians Not Taxed in the United States (Except Alaska) at the Eleventh Census: 1890* (Washington, DC: Government Printing Office, 1894), 355.

23. Stewart Culin, "Report of Archaeological and Ethnological Collecting Trips in 1901," Culin Archival Collection, Department of Ethnology, Brooklyn Museum of Art, New York. Culin left the University of Pennsylvania to become Brooklyn Museum's curator of ethnology in 1903.

24. "The Care of the Red Men. Meeting of the Women's National Indian Association," *New York Times*, December 8, 1892; "Indians and Missionaries," *New Orleans Daily Picayune*, December 7, 1897, p. 3; "Woman's Indian Association," *New Orleans Daily Picayune*, November 9, 1902, p. 15. For analysis of the association's southern chapters, see Rose Stremlau, "WNIA Chapters in the South," *Women's National Indian Association*, ed. Mathes, 173–91.

25. "Indian Missions," *Daily Picayune*, January 7, 1892, February 11, 1892; *Annual Report of the Women's National Indian Association, December, 1892* (Philadelphia: Women's National Indian Association, n.d.), 21; *New Orleans Times-Democrat*, May 12, 1893; "The Indian

Association. Aid Extended to the Aborigines," *Daily Picayune,* January 11, 1894; *Annual Report of the Women's National Indian Association, 1894* (Philadelphia: Women's National Indian Association, n.d.), 23; "Indians and Missionaries," *Daily Picayune,* December 7, 1897; "Women Defenders of Indians' Rights. The Local Association Holds Its Annual Meeting and Presents a Record of Christian Work Accomplished in the Cause of Humanity and Civilization, Not Even the War Causing the Neglect of Their Self-Appointed Mission," *Daily Picayune,* April 13, 1899; *Annual Report of the Women's National Indian Association, December, 1902* (Philadelphia: Women's National Indian Association, n.d.), 28–29.

26. *New Orleans Times-Democrat,* April 25, 1901.

27. *Annual Report of the National Indian Association, December, 1908* (New York: National Indian Association, n.d.), 18–19; *Annual Report of the National Indian Association, December, 1909* (New York: National Indian Association, n.d.), 18.

28. W. Kenneth Holditch, "'A Creature Set Apart': Pearl Rivers in the Piney Woods," in *Mississippi's Piney Woods: A Human Perspective,* ed. Noel Polk (Jackson: University Press of Mississippi, 1986), 103–20; Patricia Brady, "Eliza Jane Nicholson (1843–1896): New Orleans Publisher," in *Louisiana Women: Their Lives and Times,* ed. Janet Allured and Judith F. Gentry (Athens: University of Georgia, 2009), 94–113.

29. [Eliza Nicholson], "Indian Baskets," *Daily Picayune,* February 27, 1887.

30. "Catharine Cole Correspondence," *Daily Picayune,* October 26, 1884. Other writers in this circle of Crescent City ladies included scenes and episodes involving Indian basketry—in fiction as well as nonfiction. They include Grace King, Kate Chopin, Martha Field's daughter Flora Field, Mollie Moore Davis, and Ruth McEnery Stuart. Stuart, the most popular among these authors at the time, was an avid collector. Her collection would be purchased by the American Museum of Natural History.

31. "Catherine Cole's Letter," *Daily Picayune,* December 16, 1888, printed in Martha R. Field, *Louisiana Voyages: The Travel Writings of Catherine Cole,* ed. Joan B. McLaughlin and Jack McLaughlin (Jackson: University Press of Mississippi, 2006), 192–93.

32. C. Bremer, *The Chata Indians of Pearl River* (New Orleans: Picayune Job Print, 1907), 15 pages, with description of basketry on pp. 5–7. For additional information about the Choctaws described in Bremer's essay, see John H. Peterson Jr., "Louisiana Choctaw Life at the End of the Nineteenth Century," in *Four Centuries of Southern Indians,* ed. Charles M. Hudson (Athens: University of Georgia Press, 1975), 101–12.

33. Cora Bremer to Mary Bradford, October 25, 1902, Mary Bradford Papers.

34. Cora Bremer to Franz Boas, February 3, April 20, May 9, June 7, June 18, July 9, 1902, Accession Number 1902-50, Division of Anthropological Archives, American Museum of Natural History, New York.

35. *Sixth Biennial Report of the Board of Curators, January 1, 1916, to December 31, 1917* (New Orleans: Louisiana State Museum, 1918), 44, 77; *Annual Report of the Board of Curators for 1918* (New Orleans: Louisiana State Museum, 1919), 21, 49; *Handbook and Guide to the Louisiana State Museum* (New Orleans: Louisiana State Museum, 1934), 104.

36. Cora Bremer to Mary Bradford, December 1, 1902, Mary Bradford Papers.

37. David I. Bushnell Jr., *The Choctaw of Bayou Lacomb, St. Tammany Parish, Louisiana,* Smithsonian Institution Bureau of American Ethnology Bulletin 48 (Washington, DC: Government Printing Office, 1909), 13–15. For additional information about community members consulted by Bushnell, see Tom Mould, *Choctaw Tales* (Jackson: University Press of Mississippi, 2004), 8–10.

38. David I. Bushnell Jr. to Clark Wissler, January 17, 1916, Wissler to Bushnell, February 11, 1916, Receipt of purchase from David I. Bushnell, February 15, 1916, Accession Number 1917–10, Division of Anthropological Archives, American Museum of Natural History, New York; Handwritten list of items sold by Bushnell, American Museum of Natural History internet database; "Museum Notes," *American Museum Journal* 17 (March 1917):215.

39. David I. Bushnell Jr., "The Choctaw of St. Tammany Parish," *Louisiana Historical Quarterly* 1 (January 8, 1917): 11–20. When describing the pack basket in this essay, Bushnell referred to several examples shown in François Bernard's painting—a painting that was then in the possession of Mrs. Charles T. Yenni of New Orleans. She was the widow of Charles T. Yenni (1860–1909), well-known photographer, founder of the N.O. Photographers Association, and president of the New Orleans Levee Board from 1887 to 1909. Their address was 932 Carrolton.

40. Catherine Gardiner, on stationary of DUNARD White Star World Cruise, on board "Franconia," no date, Folder 1, Catherine Marshall Gardiner Papers, Lauren Rogers Museum of Art, Laurel, MS. For insight into Gardiner and her collection, see William Ashley Harris, "Catherine Marshall Gardiner: A Lifetime of Journey," and Betty J. Duggan, "Baskets of the Southeast," in *By Native Hands: Woven Treasure from the Lauren Rogers Museum of Art,* ed. Jill R. Chancey (Laurel, MS: Lauren Rogers Museum of Art, 2005), 10–73; and Joyce Herold, "Catherine Marshal Gardiner and Her Baskets," *American Indian Art Museum* 40 (Summer 2015): 60–69.

41. Catalog in Folder 13, Catherine Marshall Gardiner Papers.

42. Katherine M. B. Osburn, "Mississippi Choctaws and Racial Politics," *Southern Cultures* 14 (Winter 2008): 32–54. For a deep inquiry into how Native South history has been appropriated by the white South's "Lost Cause" narrative, see Gina Caison, *Red States: Indigeneity, Settler Colonialism, and Southern Studies* (Athens: University of Georgia Press, 2018).

43. Katherine M. B. Osburn, *Choctaw Resurgence in Mississippi: Race, Class, and Nation Building in the Jim Crow South, 1830–1977* (Lincoln: University of Nebraska Press, 2014), 42–47, 99; Mikaëla M. Adams, *Who Belongs? Race, Resources, and Tribal Citizenship in the Native South* (New York: Oxford University Press, 2016), 96–131; Rufus Ward, "Ask Rufus: Choctaw Baskets," *The Dispatch* (Columbus and Starkville, MS), September 17, 2018; "Choctaw Baskets Distributed from Cellar in Capital," *Washington Post,* June 3, 1928, p. 12.

44. J. Douglas Smith, "The Campaign for Racial Purity and the Erosion of Paternalism in Virginia, 1922–1930: 'Nominally White, Biologically Mixed, and Legally Negro,'" *Journal of Southern History* 68 (February 2002): 65–106; Laura J. Feller, *Being Indigenous in Jim Crow Virginia: Powhatan People and the Color Line* (Norman: University of Oklahoma Press, 2022).

45. For the Houmas' struggle for education, see Kimberly Krupa, "'So-Called Indians' Stand Up and Fight: How a Jim Crow Suit Thrust a Louisiana School System into the Civil Rights Movements," *Louisiana History* 51(Spring 2010): 171–94; Racheal Minchew, "'Because Colored Means Negro': The Houma Nation and Its Fight for Indigenous Identity within a South Louisiana Public School System, 1916–1963," M.A. thesis, University of New Orleans, 2014; and J. Daniel d'Oney, *A Kingdom of Water: Adaptation and Survival in the Houma Nation* (Lincoln: University of Nebraska Press, 2020), 79–107. For glimpses into the role played by their production of crafts, see Frank G. Speck, "A Social Reconnaissance of the Creole Houma Indian Trappers of the Louisiana Bayous, *America Indigena* 3 (1943): 134–46, 212–20; and Janel M. Curry-Roper, "Houma Blowguns and Baskets in the Mississippi River Delta," *Journal of Cultural Geography* 2 (Spring/Summer 1982): 13–22.

46. Stephanie Cole and Natalie J. Ring, eds., *The Folly of Jim Crow: Rethinking the Segregated South* (College Station: Texas A&M University Press, 2012); Jessica Barbata Jackson, *Dixie's Italians: Sicilians, Race, and Citizenship in the Jim Crow Gulf South* (Baton Rouge: Louisiana State University Press, 2020).

47. Katherine M. B. Osburn, "Mississippi Choctaws and Racial Politics," *Southern Cultures* 14 (Winter 2008): 32–54. Also see Christopher Arris Oakley on North Carolina, Brian Klopotek on Louisiana, Arica L. Coleman on Virginia, Malinda Maynor Lowery on Lumbee, and Mikäela M. Adams, *Who Belongs? Race, Resources, and Tribal Citizenship in the Native South* (New York: Oxford University Press, 2016).

48. For insight into how interaction with anthropologists and others contributed to visual and material self-representation by the Alabama-Coushattas and Coushattas, see Stephanie May de Montigny, "Chiefs, Churches, and 'Old Industries': Photographic Representations of Alabama-Coushatta and Coushatta Culture and Identity," *American Indian Culture and Research Journal* 32 (no. 4, 2008): 1–40.

CONCLUSION

1. Angela Gonzales, Judy Kertész, and Gabrielle Tayac, "Eugenics as Indian Removal: Sociohistorical Processes and the De(con)struction of American Indians in the Southeast," *The Public Historian* 29 (Summer 2007): 53–67.

2. Denise E. Bates, *The Other Movement: Indian Rights and Civil Rights in the Deep South* (Tuscaloosa: University of Alabama Press, 2012); Mark Edwin Miller, *Claiming Tribal Identity: The Five Tribes and the Politics of Federal Acknowledgment* (Norman: University of Oklahoma Press, 2013).

3. Other state-recognized tribes are the Adai Caddo Indians of Louisiana, the Biloxi Chitimacha Confederation/Bayou Lafourche Band, the Biloxi Chitimacha Confederation/Grand Caillou/Dulac Band, the Four-Winds Cherokee Tribe, the Louisiana Band of Choctaw Indians, the Point au Chien Tribe, and the Natchitoches Tribe of Louisiana. See Federal and State-Tribal Contact Information, Louisiana Governor's Office of Indian Affairs, https://gov.louisiana.gov/assets/docs/Indian-Affairs/LouisianaTribalList.

4. Georgann Eubanks, *Saving the Wild South: The Fight for Native Plants on the Brink of Extinction* (Chapel Hill: University of North Carolina Press, 2021), 3, 166–76. For essential guidance into the various cane basketry and rivercane restoration projects underway, see Dayna Bowker Lee and H. F. Gregory, *The Work of Tribal Hands: Southeastern Indian Split Cane Basketry* (Natchitoches, LA: Northwestern State University Press, 2006). For basketry's connection with language recovery, see George Morris, "Language: Chitimachas Working to Revive Their Lost Tribal Language," *Baton Rouge Advocate,* November 25, 2007; Larry Abramson, "Software Company Helps Revive 'Sleeping Language.'" All Things Considered, National Public Radio, aired on February 2, 2010; Daniel W. Hieber, "Reborn on the Bayou: A Lost Language of Louisiana," *Houston Chronicle,* July 28, 2015, and "The Chitimacha Language: A History," in *Language in Louisiana: Community and Culture,* ed. Nathalie Dajko and Shana Walton (Jackson: University Press of Mississippi, 2019), 9–27. The relationship between basketry and language is playing out in several places across Indian country. In northern California the Yuroks have constructed on Blue Creek near Klamath a gathering place that includes a space for dancing and praying along with a plank house for basket weavers to teach and demonstrate their craft. Restoration of the Yurok language is a central objective in this cultural program. Patricia Leigh Brown, "A Vision of Reviving Tribal Ways in a Remote Corner of California," *New York Times,* March 18, 2012.

5. Lisa Snell, "World of Norma Howard," *Native Peoples* (July–August 2015); Theresa Barbaro, "Sarah Sense: Weaving Place and Memory," *American Indian* 15 (Spring 2014): 18–25; Theresa Barbaro, "Shan Goshorn: Re-Weaving History," *American Indian* 15 (Summer/Fall 2014): 22–35; Tasiyagnunpa Livermont, "Cultural Burdens: A Tribute to Native Women," *Native Peoples* (July/August 2016): 56–57; Jolene Rickard, "Visualizing Sovereignty in the Time of Biometric Sensors," *South Atlantic Quarterly* 110 (Spring 2011): 465–82, quote from 474.

6. "Notes from the Council Table," *Chitimacha Tribe of Louisiana Newsletter* (September 2016), 2; Sarah Kaplan, "In Museum Archives, a Louisiana Tribe Urgently Seeks Proof of Its Past," *New Orleans Times-Picayune,* November 11, 2017.

7. Jill Ahlberg Yohe and Teri Greeves, *Hearts of Our People: Native Women Artists* [catalog] (Minneapolis Institute of Art in association with the University of Washington Press, 2019), 55–56.

8. B. W. Merwin, "Basketry of the Chitimacha Indians: A Gift from Mrs. William Pepper," *Museum Journal* 10(no. 1, 1919), 29–34. For information about Edward Avery McIlhenny's expedition to Alaska for the University of Pennsylvania's museum and the collection that he assembled, see Lucy Fowler Williams, *Guide to the North American Ethnographic Collections at the University of Pennsylvania Museum of Archaeology and Anthropology* (Philadelphia: University of Pennsylvania Museum of Archaeology and Anthropology, 2003), 5–6.

9. Christine DeLucia, Doug Kiel, Katrina Phillips, and Klara Vigil, "Histories of Indigenous Sovereignty in Action: What Is It and Why Does It Matter?" *American Historian* (March 2021): 20–31, quote from 22.

10. Rayna Green, "The Pocahontas Perplex: The Image of Indian Women in American Culture," *Massachusetts Review* 16 (Autumn 1975): 698–714; John Shelton Reed, "The Cherokee Princess in the Family Tree," *Southern Cultures* 3 (Spring 1997): 111–13.

11. Clara Sue Kidwell, "Indian Women as Cultural Mediators," *Ethnohistory* 39 (Spring 1992): 97–107. For astute analysis of what recent weaponization of the Pocahontas myth reveals about the persistence of colonial violence, see Kevin Bruyneel, *Settler Memory: The Disavowal of indigeneity and the Politics of Race in the United States* (Chapel Hill: University of North Carolina Press, 2021), 146–55.

INDEX